GREAT CREPE RECIPES

By Rose-Marie Brooks

Dorison House Publishers, Inc., New York

Copyright © 1976 by Sunbeam Corporation

Published by Dorison House Publishers, Inc.
183 Madison Avenue, New York, N.Y. 10016

ISBN: 0-916752-03-8

Library of Congress Catalog Card Number: 76-295-14

Manufactured in the United States of America

TABLE OF CONTENTS

A Crepe By Every Other Name

The Russians call them blinchiki or blini and they serve them with caviar. The Italians make them into that delight called cannelloni. Lovers of Chinese food order them as crisp egg rolls or eat them plain, wrapped around delicacies like Moo Shoo Pork. And, for festive occasions, the French created that flaming fantasy, Crepes Suzette.

In fact, every nation seems to have a marvelous crepe dish. Call for a Hungarian palacsinta, a Jewish blintz, a Scandinavian platter or a Mexican enchilada; call for crepes by any other name and enjoy a food that is different and delicious.

Crepes are among the most versatile dishes ever conceived. They can be served at breakfast, lunch, dinner or for late-night supper. They can be served hot or cold. Serve crepes as an appetizer, a main dish, a vegetable, in soup or as a dessert. Stuff them with hearty fillings or delicate mixtures. Freeze them, and always be ready when friends and family want a treat.

Master the making of crepes and you'll win the reputation of being a fabulous cook. It's simple; crepes are as easy to make as they are elegant to serve. That's because they are nothing more than thin, flexible pancakes made from a few basic ingredients — eggs, milk, flour — and cooked in or "on" a very hot frying pan.

It's what you do with crepes that makes them exciting. For fillings, use whatever you have available, plus your imagination. Experiment and enjoy.

Crepe Makers

With the advent of the electrically controlled dipping pan, the art of making crepes has become so simple that no matter how limited your experience in the kitchen, you can have superb results every time.

The M'sieur Crepe Electric Crepe Maker's controlled heat, "cook on the bottom of the pan" method makes everyone into a skilled crepemaker because it produces perfectly finished crepes every time.

While the recipes in this book were developed especially for the M'sieur Crepe 7-1/2 inch pan, they can be adapted to other electric pans, inside bakers (skillets) and bottom bakers (domed griddles). These pans come in a variety of sizes from small (5 to 6 inches) to large (up to 8 inches). Bottom bakers are dipped and the crepes are usually thinner, yielding a greater number of crepes than specified in some batter recipes. Batter is poured into the skillet baker, a small pan taking 2 to 3 tablespoons for each crepe and a large pan taking 3 to 4 tablespoons.

BOTTOM BAKERS
THE DIP-AND-BAKE METHOD OF BAKING CREPES

Step one
Dip preheated pan into batter in 9-inch pie pan for seconds. Gently lift and turn over.

Step two
Return pan to heat immediately and cook until edge of crepe shows slight browning.

Step three
Remove from heat. Turn pan over and gently loosen edge of crepe with plastic or wooden spatula. Crepe should loosen easily but some heavier batters might require loosening center of crepe with spatula.

Step four
Stack crepes on platter.

INSIDE BAKERS
THE SKILLET METHOD OF BAKING CREPES

Step one
Brush pan with oil or butter if it does not have a non-stick coating. Heat pan over medium-high heat.

Step two
Lift heated pan from heating unit and pour in batter (2 to 3 tablespoons in a small pan, 3 to 4 tablespoons in a large pan) tilting the pan in all directions and swirling batter to cover pan in a very thin layer.

Step three
Return to heating unit. Cook over medium-high heat until bottom is browned lightly and top of crepe is dry.

Step four
Carefully turn crepe with plastic or Teflon-coated spatula and brown other side for a few seconds.

Step Five
Remove from pan with spatula and stack on platter. The second side is rarely as browned as the first. It should be used as the "inside" of the crepe.

Features Of The M'sieur Crepe Crepe Maker

Crepe
Pan

Heating
Plate

Heat
Control
Knob

Heating Base

Before Using
The M'sieur Crepe Crepe Maker

Before using the M' SIEUR CREPE crepe maker for the first time, wash the crepe pan in warm soapy water, using a soft sponge or dishcloth. Rinse pan thoroughly and dry. DO NOT IMMERSE HEATING BASE IN WATER.

Place crepe maker unit on a flat, level surface. Set dial on heat control knob to the "OFF" position. Arrange the electrical cord so that it is not wrapped around the crepe maker base and does not touch heated surfaces. Plug electrical cord into 120 volt, 60 Hz AC wall outlet. AVOID MOVING CREPE MAKER AFTER IT IS PLUGGED IN AND HEATED.

Caution:

1. Pots and pans other than the crepe pan provided are not to be used on the crepe maker heating base.

2. Food should not be placed directly on the crepe maker heating base.

3. The crepe pan is designed to be used only on the crepe maker heating base, *not* for stove top cooking.

To Use The M'sieur Crepe Crepe Maker

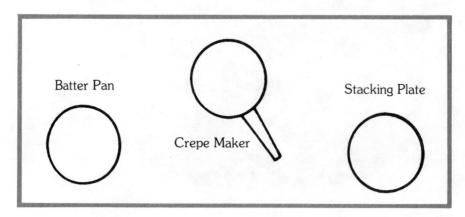

Batter Pan

Stacking Plate

Crepe Maker

Kitchen Countertop

Prepare the basic crepe batter recipe of your choice and pour it into a shallow 9-inch metal pie pan. Cover the batter. ALLOW THE BATTER TO STAND AT ROOM TEMPERATURE APPROXIMATELY ONE HOUR. Arrange the crepe maker, batter, and a stacking plate on the kitchen countertop as shown. This arrangement will give you the most efficient operating method.

Remove the crepe pan from the heating base and lightly coat the bottom surface with cooking oil or margarine. Apply oil or margarine using a pastry brush, then wipe with a paper towel to remove excess oil. This will "condition" the no-stick cooking surface. CAUTION: DO NOT APPLY OIL TO THE HEATING PLATE.

Set the heat control knob on the crepe maker to the low end of the "CREPE" range. Temperatures at this setting may need to be set higher depending on the desired brownness of the crepe and the desired cooking time.

Place the crepe pan in an inverted position on the heating plate. (A)

For best results, preheat the crepe maker unit for 4 minutes before starting to make crepes. Too long a preheat time may cause the crepe pan to be too hot and the first crepe may be lost by slipping back into the pan of batter.

Dip the heated pan bottom no more than 1/4 inch into the crepe batter. Tilting slightly when dipping the pan will minimize the chance of trapping air in the batter, which results in holes in the crepes.

Hold the pan in the batter for 3 to 4 seconds, coating the entire bottom of the pan. (B) If the bottom of the pan is not completely coated or has holes, do not dip the pan back into the batter.

(A)

(B)

After dipping the crepe pan in the batter, lift the pan and tilt to a vertical position. Hold the pan in this position, allowing any excess batter to drip back into the metal pie pan. (C)

Place the crepe pan in an inverted position (bottom side facing up) on the heating base and allow to bake for 1 to 1-1/2 minutes. (D)

The crepe has finished baking when the batter no longer steams or bubbles, and is delicately browned around the edges. (Approximately 1 to 1-1/2 minutes.) The underside of the crepe will be a light tan color. The top side of the crepe *will not* have a tan color. It is not necessary to bake both sides of the crepe, as the lighter side is filled and folded inward.

Using a fork, gently loosen the browned edges of the crepe. (E) Lift the pan from the heating base. Invert pan and remove the crepe onto a stacking plate. (F)

When the crepe batter is getting low in the metal pie pan, tilt the pan slightly to help cover the bottom of the crepe pan. There may be some remaining batter in the pie pan that will not be able to be reached.

(C)

(D)

Crepes may be prepared in advance, layered between wax paper, and wrapped in aluminum foil for freezing. To freeze, place a crepe on a sheet of wax paper. Be sure to flatten out each crepe as it is layered on the wax paper. It is best to maintain an even stack of crepes, to prevent uneven edges which may become brittle and break in the freezer. Wrap the stack of crepes in aluminum foil and freeze. Some crepe fillings may be prepared in advance and refrigerated or frozen for later use. After removing the stack of crepes from the freezer, allow the crepes to thaw enough to separate, then continue thawing until the individual crepes are soft and pliable for easy filling and folding. If desired, crepes can be wrapped in aluminum foil and warmed in the oven at a low temperature (200° F.) Remove wax paper layers before warming.

For best results, prepare, fill, fold, and serve the crepes or prepare, stack, wrap, and freeze the crepes.

NOTE: If crepe batter accidentally drops onto the heating plate, turn the unit "OFF" and disconnect from outlet. Allow unit to cool. Using a metal spatula, carefully scrape off the spilled batter. Cooking performance will be hindered if batter is allowed to remain on the heating plate. Connect crepe maker to electrical outlet and begin process again.

(E)

(F)

Additional Uses

The M'SIEUR CREPE crepe maker pan may be used as a convenient small frypan when used on the crepe maker heating base. This small frypan can be used for frying hamburgers, sausages, and bacon; scrambling or frying one or two eggs; and sauteing mushrooms, onions, and other vegetables.

To Use The Frypan

Thoroughly wash the frypan in warm, soapy water, especially the side used for making crepes. Condition the inside surface of the frypan by wiping with cooking oil or margarine. Remove excess oil with a paper towel.

Set heat control knob to the "OFF" position and plug the crepe maker into a 120 volt, 60 Hz AC outlet.

To set temperature, rotate the heat control knob to the "FRYING" setting at the point recommended in the fry guide (See page 13).

Preheat the frypan if recommended in the fry guide. Add food or recommended amount of shortening. Tilt frypan slightly to coat the entire surface with shortening. Fry food as directed in the fry guide.

When cooking is completed, turn heat control knob to "OFF" and remove plug from electrical outlet.

Care And Cleaning

Avoid digging into the no-stick finish or cutting the surface of the crepe pan with a sharp knife or utensil. Use a "light touch" with metal cooking utensils. Light or fine scratches on the no-stick cooking surface seldom affect the release properties of the surface. Such damage is really a matter of appearance and not performance.

To clean, wash the crepe pan in hot, soapy water. Be sure to remove any oils from the inside and outside surfaces of the pan. Oils will eventually build up, causing the finish to stain or to lose its release properties. Rubbing the pan briskly with a plastic scrubber or stiff sponge will help remove built-up oils and food residues.

CAUTION: DO NOT USE METAL SCOURING PADS FOR CLEANING AS THEY WILL DAMAGE THE COOKING SURFACE OF THE PAN. METAL PIECES OF THE PADS CAN BREAK OFF AND MAY CAUSE ELECTRICAL HAZARDS.

Rinse crepe pan thoroughly and dry. Wipe outside of the cool crepe maker with a damp cloth and dry.

To protect fine furniture, do not use crepe maker on unprotected surfaces. Damage to the surface could occur during heating.

Storage

Do not store or place the crepe maker unit in an oven. Oven temperatures will damage plastic parts of the base. The electrical cord may be loosely wound around the base of the crepe maker. ONLY AFTER THE CREPE MAKER BASE IS COOL.

Fry Guide

Food	Setting In Fry Range	Time	Instructions
Bacon	Medium	9 min.	Do not preheat. Cut bacon slices in half. Arrange bacon slices in frypan. Avoid overcrowding. Fry, turning occasionally, until crisp as desired. Drain on paper toweling.
Eggs-Fried 1 egg)	Low	2-3 min.	Preheat frypan. Add 1 teaspoon fat. Add egg. Fry until done as desired. Remove with pancake turner.
Eggs Scrambled (2 eggs)	Low	1 min.	Preheat frypan. Add 2 teaspoons fat. Break 2 eggs into bowl, add 2 tablespoons milk, salt and pepper to taste. Beat lightly. Carefully pour mixture into hot pan. When mixture begins to set at sides and bottom, gently stir with a fork until cooked as desired.
French Toast (2 slices)	Medium	3-5 min.	Combine 1 egg, 1/3 cup milk, 1/4 teaspoon vanilla in a small bowl. Beat with a fork until well blended. Preheat frypan. Add 2 tablespoons butter. Dip slice of bread into egg mixture, only until coated. Fry until browned on both sides.
Hamburgers (3 at 1/4 lb. each)	High	15 min.	Prepare burger patties. Preheat frypan. Add burgers. Brown on each side and continue cooking until desired doneness.
Sausage (5 links)	Low	25 min.	Do not preheat. Arrange sausage links or patties in frypan. Set heat control and fry until browned and no pink color remains. Turn frequently with tongs. Brown pre-cooked sausages following directions on package label.
Vegetables (1 cup)	Medium	1-3 min	Slice or cut to desired size pieces. Preheat pan. Melt 1 tablespoon butter or margarine. Add vegetables. Cook and stir until desired doneness.

Shaping The Crepe

The shape of your crepe depends on the filling you are using and how you want the finished crepe to look. Start off with the attractive browner side (one side is inevitably better looking than the other) on the outside and fold as the recipe suggests or as you please.

The following are a few of the most popular folds:

Traditional or Fold-Over
This most popular of shapes is excellent for entree or dessert recipes. To fold, place the crepe flat, spoon or spread filling along center of crepe. Fold one side over to cover filling. Fold opposite side to overlap first fold. Ends are left open to show off filling.

Half or Single Fold
This is an excellent fold for drier fillings and fillings that are too large for other shapes. To fold, place crepe flat, and put filling on half of it. Fold other side over.

Spiral Roll or Roll-Up
This is a good choice for fillings that are spreadable. To fold, place crepe flat, spread filling over surface and start rolling tightly from one end like a jelly roll. Make into bite-size appetizers by cutting into 4 or 5 small sections.

Triangle or Quarter Fold
This is the classic Crepe Suzette fold. To use with fillings, place crepe flat and spoon small amount of filling in center. Fold in half and fold in half again to form a triangle four layers thick.

Blintz or Fry Fold
This is the fold for crepes that are to be sauteed or deep fried. The filling should be placed on the browner side of the crepe. Place crepe flat and spoon filling on center. Fold bottom over to cover half of filling; then fold right side over slightly more than half of filling and left side to overlap. Fold top of crepe to center, covering folds.

Pocket Roll
This is an excellent fold for runny fillings or fillings that should be heated. The sides are folded to keep the mixture inside the crepe. To fold, place crepe flat, and spoon filling on, leaving at least a half-inch border around crepe. Fold right and left sides inward to cover 1/3 filling on either side. Start rolling from bottom, keeping folded sides tucked in. Heat and serve fold side down.

Basket Fold
This is an unusual fold. Use small crepes or trim large one to fit in muffin pan. Tuck crepes best side up into greased cups, arranging tops into interesting shapes. Fill and bake.

Layering or Stacking
This makes an attractive dessert or appetizer. Spread each layer with filling and stack to desired height. Cut in pie-shape wedges to serve.

Guide To Folding Crepes

When served, crepes are folded to enclose the desired filling. For each crepe recipe in this book, a recommended fold to use is given. Below are the most common folds used when serving crepes.

Traditional Fold

Spiral Roll

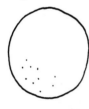

Fry Fold

To seal the seam and brown the crepe—place the crepe into hot oil, folded edge down.

Triangle Fold

Layering

Making The Crepe Perfect

Every good cook knows that perfection is a matter of correction. Problems do come up but for almost every problem there's a solution. Here's how to make your crepes perfect.

Problem	Cause	Solution
Sticking	Heat too low	Increase temperature
	Batter too thin	Thicken with flour
	Pan not oiled or seasoned correctly	Oil and season as directed on page
	Pan not properly cleaned	Cool pan. Wash, dry and oil
Brittleness and Cracking	Batter too thin	Thicken with flour
	Pan too hot	Cool pan and lower temperature
Holes	Trapped air under batter	Dip knife into batter and patch holes if crepe is to be used for frying. However, holes are not undesirable and usually cause no problem.
Not Browning	Pan too cool	Preheat pan longer or increase temperature
Batter Slips Back into Dipping Pan	Pan too hot	Cool pan and lower temperature
	Pan pulled from batter too quickly	Leave pan in batter at least 3 to 4 seconds
Tiny Lumps	Batter not blended	Strain batter through sieve.
Batter too Thick	Too little liquid	Add tablespoon or more of liquid until batter is proper consistency
Bubbles	Flour not expanded	Let batter stand for 1 hour before baking

Cooking For The Future

Crepes are delicate creations but they have a durable nature. Unfilled crepes freeze easily, take little space in the freezer and defrost without loss of taste and quality if kept not more than six to eight weeks.

So don't worry about extras when you're cooking. Save them for future dinners, snacks or unexpected guests. Or prepare ahead for dinners and parties.

To freeze crepes:

Stack crepes with a piece of waxed paper between each one. Wrap in packages of eight, ten or twelve, depending on the number usually required by your family, in foil, freezer wrap or plastic bags sealed at the end.

Many filled crepes may also be frozen. The best results are obtained with those that have tomato sauces or drier mixtures. Fillings with sauces containing flour or eggs generally do not freeze well. Gelatin mixtures cannot be frozen. Many herbs and spices will lose their flavor.

To freeze filled crepes:

Place crepes in pan in which they will be baked when defrosted. Wrap in foil, freezer wrap or plastic freezer bags.

When you are ready to use them, unwrap and let stand at room temperature for an hour. Bake in oven at 375° F. for about an hour. If crepes are fully defrosted, baking time is reduced to 30 minutes. Dot with butter or add sauce before placing in oven.

Metric Measures

"Going metric" means more than just converting to the language of the new measures; it means a change in standards. An American National Standards Institute subcommittee (the group responsible for standardizing customary measures, such as a cup) is currently working to standardize the new metric measures. Since measures are not really equivalent, you will need new measuring cups, spoons, etc. Where measures are marked in both customary and metric units they are not always accurate.

While all recipes in this book have been given in metric measures as well as customary units, the recipes were developed with customary units and may require some slight adjustment — probably not more than a 5% increase.

THE BATTERS

FOR MAIN DISHES:

Basic Entree Crepes I
Basic Entree Crepes II
Beer Crepes
Cornmeal Crepes
Nutty Crepes
Oatmeal Crepes
Onion Crepes
Potato Crepes
Rye Crepes
Whole Wheat Crepes

FOR DESSERTS:

Basic Dessert Crepes
Chocolate Crepes
Cinnamon-Nut Dessert

MAKING THE BATTER—THE FIRST STEP

One of the truisms of great cooking is that the most exciting dishes in the world are made from the simplest ingredients.

The elegant crepe is one of these dishes.

The basic crepe is made from eggs, milk, flour and butter in proportions of 1/2 cup flour and 1/2 cup liquid to one egg, with butter added for richness and flavor.

More flour will thicken the batter, more liquid will thin it. The liquid need not be milk. Try making crepes with water, juice, broth or cream. Herbs and spices add flavor and taste. The variations are endless, and most creative crepe makers eventually develop recipes of their own.

Essentially crepes fall into two basic categories: entree and dessert. Entree crepes are used to wrap meat, vegetables and appetizers, and are made from a variety of flour grains. Dessert crepes are usually sweeter and are served with luscious rich and creamy fillings, sweet sauces or aflame in liqueur.

The batter recipes in this book offer you a choice of crepes to complement the more than 200 fillings for which we've included recipes.

Each batter has an individual look and taste. Some ingredients will result in a slightly thicker or more textured batter. Some batters have a tendency to brown faster. Some batters should be thinned as you cook. Depending on the thickness of your crepes and the textures of the batter, the yield may vary, but all batters in this book have been developed to produce a minimum of 12 to 14 crepes.

TO MIX THE BATTER

Use an Electric Mixer

The mixer is especially good with smooth and delicately textured batters such as cornmeal or whole wheat.

To mix: Beat eggs. Add liquid and salt. Beat at medium speed, gradually adding flour until all ingredients are combined. Stir in seasonings or flavorings, if any.

Use a Blender

The blender provides the quickest and easiest method of blending smooth and heavy textured batters, such as those containing nuts, potatoes and crackers.

To Blend: Combine all ingredients in blender. Blend about 30 seconds. Scrape down sides and stir batter. Blend 15 seconds more.

Use a Wire Whisk or Rotary Beater

Mixing by hand is, of course, more strenuous and time consuming than using an electric mixer or blender, but it is just as effective. If making a basic smooth batter you will probably have to strain to remove tiny lumps.

To Mix: Beat eggs. Add half the liquid and gradually add flour, beating constantly until smooth. Gradually add remaining liquid. Strain to remove lumps. Stir in seasonings, if any.

FOR MAIN DISHES:

CHOOSING THE CREPE
Two basic batters for light rich crepes

ENTREE CREPES I

---

4 eggs
1 cup (240 ml)
1/2 cup (120 ml) milk
1/2 teaspoon (2.5 ml) salt

1/2 cup (120 ml) chicken
  or beef stock
1 tablespoon (15 ml) melted
  margarine or butter

flour?

Yield: 12 to 14 crepes

Mix with Mixer

Measure all ingredients except flour into large mixing bowl. Gradually add flour, beating with electric mixer until smooth. Cover batter and let stand at room temperature one hour before baking.

Mix with Blender

Measure all ingredients into blender jar; blend for about 30 seconds. Scrape down sides with rubber spatula. Blend 15 seconds more or until smooth. Cover batter and let stand at room temperature one hour before baking.

Mix with Whisk or Rotary Beater

Beat eggs in large mixing bowl. Add all remaining ingredients except flour. Gradually add flour, beating with rotary beater or using whisk, until smooth. If tiny lumps remain, strain. Cover batter and let stand at room temperature one hour before baking.

ENTREE CREPES II

---

2 eggs, beaten
1/2 cup (120 ml) milk
1/2 cup (120 ml) cold water

1 cup (240 ml) unsifted flour
1 tablespoon (15 ml)
  melted butter

Yield: 12 to 14 crepes

Mix with Mixer

Measure all ingredients except flour into large mixing bowl. Gradually add flour, beating with electric mixer until smooth. Cover batter and let stand at room temperature one hour before baking.

Mix with Blender

Measure all ingredients into blender jar; blend for about 30 seconds. Scrape down sides with rubber spatula. Blend 15 seconds more, or until smooth. Cover batter and let stand at room temperature one hour before baking.

Mix with Whisk or Rotary Beater

Beat eggs in large mixing bowl. Add all remaining ingredients except flour. Gradually add flour, beating with rotary beater or using whisk, until smooth. If tiny lumps remain, strain. Cover batter and let stand at room temperature one hour before baking.

BEER CREPE BATTER

3 eggs
1 cup (240 ml) beer
1/2 teaspoon (2.5 ml) salt

1 cup (240 ml) unsifted flour
1-1/2 tablespoons (125 ml)
   butter, melted

Yield: 12 to 14 crepes

With electric mixer, beat eggs, stir in beer and salt. Gradually add flour, beating until batter is smooth. Stir in melted butter. Let batter stand about 1 hour before baking.

CORNMEAL CREPES

3/4 cup (180 ml) flour
1/2 cup (120 ml) cornmeal
1/2 cup (120 ml) water
1/2 teaspoon (2.5 ml) salt

2 tablespoons (30 ml) melted
   butter or margarine
2 teaspoons (10 ml) sugar
1 teaspoon (5 ml) vanilla

Yield: 12 to 14 crepes

Measure all ingredients except flour into large mixing bowl. Beat with electric mixer on medium speed, gradually add flour, until all ingredients are combined. If small lumps are present, pour batter through strainer.

NUTTY CREPE BATTER

3 eggs
2 cups (480 ml) milk
1-1/4 cup (300 ml) flour
1/2 cup (120 ml) wheat germ

1/4 cup (60 ml) ground
   or very finely chopped
   pecans or walnuts
1/4 teaspoon (1.5 ml) salt

Yield: 12 to 14 crepes

Measure all ingredients into blender container, blend about 45 seconds. Scrape sides of container and blend another 15 seconds, or until mixed. Cover batter and let rest at room temperature 1 hour before cooking. Stir batter before each dipping.

Note: Stirring helps prevent settling of wheat germ and nuts. The last few crepes may be slightly thicker than the rest.

OATMEAL CREPE BATTER

3 eggs
1-1/4 cups (300 ml) milk
2 tablespoons (30 ml) melted butter
  or margarine

3/4 cup (180 ml) flour
1 1-ounce envelope (30 ml)
  instant oatmeal
1/2 teaspoon (2.5 ml) salt

Yield: 12 to 14 crepes

Measure all ingredients into blender container. Blend about 45 seconds. Scrape sides of container. Blend another 15 seconds, or until mixed. Cover batter and let rest at room temperature one hour before cooking. Stir batter before each dipping.

Note: Stirring helps prevent settling of oatmeal.

ONION CREPE BATTER

1 onion, about 2-inch
  diameter, chopped
1 tablespoon (15 ml) butter
  or margarine
2 eggs

1 cup (240 ml) milk
1 cup (240 ml) flour
1/4 teaspoon (1.5 ml) salt
Dash white pepper

Yield: 12 to 14 crepes

Saute onion in butter in frypan until tender but not brown. Combine eggs and milk in blender. Add onion. Blend. Add remaining ingredients and blend until smooth. Let stand 1 hour before baking.

POTATO CREPE BATTER

4 eggs
1 cup (240 ml) milk
3/4 cup (180 ml) seasoned
  mashed potatoes

3/4 cup (180 ml) flour
2 tablespoons (30 ml) melted butter
  or margarine

Yield: 12 to 14 crepes

Measure all ingredients (except butter) into blender container. Blend about 45 seconds. Scrape sides of container. Add butter and blend another 15 seconds, or until mixed. Cover batter and let rest at room temperature 1 hour before cooking. Stir batter before each dipping.

Note: Crepes are very tender. Stack between layers of wax paper.

RYE CREPE BATTER

Rye toast snack crackers
3 eggs
2 cups (480 ml) milk

1-1/4 cups (300 ml) flour
1/4 teaspoon (1.5 ml) salt

Yield: 12 to 14 crepes

Grind enough rye crackers in blender to make 1/2 cup. Return cracker crumbs to blender, add remaining ingredients. Blend about 45 seconds. Scrape sides of container. Blend another 15 seconds, or until mixed. Cover batter and let rest at room temperature one hour before cooking. Stir batter before each dipping.

Note: Stirring helps prevent settling of cracker crumbs.

WHOLE WHEAT CREPES

4 eggs
1 cup (240 ml) whole
wheat flour
1/2 cup (120 ml) milk
1/2 cup (120 ml) water

1/2 teaspoon (2.5 ml) salt
2 tablespoons (30 ml) melted margarine
or butter
2 teaspoons (10 ml) wheat germ

Yield: 12 to 14 crepes

Measure all ingredients into large mixing bowl. Beat with electric mixer until all ingredients are combined. It will be necessary to stir batter occasionally when making crepes, since the wheat germ tends to sink.

Textured Batters

Textured batters should be stirred between each dipping to prevent settling. To insure complete coverage for each crepe, dip; hold and invert batter pan for 1-2 seconds.

FOR DESSERTS:

BASIC DESSERT CREPES

4 eggs
1 cup (240 ml) flour
1/2 cup (120 ml) milk
1/2 cup (120 ml) water

1/2 teaspoon (2.5 ml) salt
2 tablespoons (30 ml) melted margarine
   or butter
2 teaspoons (10 ml) sugar
1 teaspoon (5 ml) vanilla

Yield: 12 to 14 crepes

Measure all ingredients except flour into large mixing bowl. Beat with electric mixer on medium speed, gradually adding flour, until all ingredients are combined. If small lumps are present, pour batter through strainer. Pour batter into a 9-inch metal pie pan.

Variation:

CHOCOLATE CREPES

Add 2 tablespoons (30 ml) chocolate sauce to above recipe.

CINNAMON-NUT DESSERT

3 eggs
1-1/2 cups (360 ml) flour
2 tablespoons (30 ml) melted butter
   or margarine
1 tablespoon (15 ml) honey

1-1/2 cups (360 ml) flour
1/4 cup (60 ml) ground or very
   finely chopped almonds
1/4 teaspoon (1.5 ml) cinnamon
1/2 teaspoon (2.5 ml) vanilla

Yield: 12 to 14 crepes

Measure all ingredients into blender container, blend about 45 seconds. Scrape sides of container and blend another 15 seconds, or until mixed. Cover batter and let rest at room temperature 1 hour before cooking. Stir batter before each dipping.

Note: Stirring helps prevent settling of nuts.

APPETIZERS AND HORS d'OEUVRE

Caponata Sicilian
Chicken Liver Crepes
Chinese Egg Roll Appetizers
Cream Cheese and Olive Roll-Ups
Crepes Oysters Rockefeller
Crispy Cheese Crepes
Dip Chips and Caviar
Fried Spinach Hors d'Oeuvre
Guacamole Appetizers
Ham Crepes Mexicana
Hot Chicken Crepes
Liederkranz Triangles

Lots of "Lox" Roll-Ups
Mushroom Hors d'Oeuvre
Nutty Blue Cheese Roll-Ups
Russian Blini
Saganaki (Greek Food for the Gods)
Shrimp Rissoles
Shrimp Toast
Snack Stack
Spicy Indian Crepes
Sweet Spice Appetizer
Taco Delights

IN THE BEGINNING ... SERVE CREPES

Crepes for appetizers or hors d'oeuvre?
Of course!

Crepes may change your entire way of planning for a dinner or a party.

Hot or cold, made in a variety of interesting shapes, served at the table as a prelude to the meal or on trays as finger food for a party, crepes are different and delectable.

Be adventuresome in choosing or creating fillings.

Try new combinations of ingredients. Add herbs and spices to your crepe bottoms. Roll the crepes in unusual shapes. The spiral roll is excellent for cold appetizers that are to be cut into bite-size pieces as well as for popping into the oven to bake or broil. A crepe stack is an eye-catching and elegant centerpiece on a buffet table.

Garnishes are important. Crepes have no color of their own and such colorful additions as parsley, watercress, strips of pimiento, green pepper or carrot, chopped egg yoke, sliced olives, small gherkins sliced lengthwise several times to spread out like a fan, or paper-thin slices of lemon or lime gently flattened, makes an appetizer tray or hors d'oeuvre plate more festive.

We suggest that you serve one crepe to each person as an hors d'oeuvre and plan on 1 to 1½ crepe for each person when serving bite-size appetizers (one crepe can be cut into 4 or 5 pieces).

CAPONATA SICILIAN

1 large eggplant, unpeeled	10 large green olives,
Salt and pepper to taste	pitted and chopped
2 medium onions, chopped	3 tablespoons (45 ml) pine nuts
1 large clove of garlic, pressed	3 tablespoons (45 ml) capers
3 celery stalks, chopped	1/4 cup (60 ml) wine vinegar
1 pound can (455 g)	2 tablespoons (30 ml) sugar
Italian plum tomatoes	1/4 teaspoon (1.5 ml) oregano

8 crepes

Wash eggplant and cut into small cubes. Season with salt and pepper. In frypan, fry in hot oil until tender. Remove and set aside. Saute onions in the same oil. Add garlic, celery, tomatoes and olives. Cook for 10 minutes over a low flame. Add eggplant, pine nuts and capers. Heat vinegar, stir in sugar and add to mixture. Cook for an additional 5 to 10 minutes. Spoon mixture onto crepe. Sprinkle with oregano. Fold. Chill before serving. Slice each crepe in 3 or 4 pieces. Garnish with parsley or thin slices of black olive.

Makes 24 to 30 pieces.
SUGGESTED CREPE BATTER: ENTREE I
SUGGESTED CREPE FOLD: SPIRAL

CHICKEN LIVER CREPES

4 slices bacon
1-1/2 pound (680 g) chicken livers
1 cup (240 ml) sliced
    fresh mushrooms
2 tablespoons (30 ml) finely
    chopped scallion or onion
10-1/2 ounce can (300 g) cream
    of chicken soup, undiluted
1/2 teaspoon (2.5 ml)
    lemon juice
Salt and pepper
2 tablespoons (30 ml) milk
1/2 cup (120ml)
    grated Swiss cheese

8 crepes

Fry bacon, drain on paper towels and set aside. Fry chicken livers, mushrooms and scallion in bacon drippings. Chop livers, return to skillet. Crumble bacon and add to ingredients. Stir in 1/2 can soup; add lemon juice, and season to taste. Spoon filling onto crepes; fold and place in greased baking dish. Stir milk into remaining soup and pour over crepes: sprinkle with grated cheese. Bake at 375°F. (190°C.) for 15 minutes, until hot and lightly browned. Garnish with thinly sliced raw mushroom and watercress.

Makes 8 individual servings.
SUGGESTED CREPE BATTER: ENTREE II
SUGGESTED CREPE FOLD: TRADITIONAL

CHINESE EGG ROLL APPETIZERS

2 tablespoons (30 ml) margarine
2 tablespoons (30 ml) green
    onions, minced
1 cup (240 ml) celery, minced
2 tablespoons (30 ml) soy sauce
1 tablespoon (15 ml) sherry
4 oz. can (115 g) shrimp, chopped
1 tablespoon (15 ml)
    cornstarch
1 pound can (455 g) bean sprouts,
    rinsed and drained
1/4 cup (60 ml) chopped spinach,
    cooked and drained
6 water chestnuts, chopped

6 to 8 crepes

Saute onion and celery in margarine. Add soy sauce, sherry, shrimp, bean sprouts, spinach and water chestnuts. Mix cornstarch with 2 tablespoons water and blend in. Cook until mixture thickens. Cool. Spoon onto crepe. Fold and tuck. Fry in 1 inch of oil, open end down, until crepe becomes browned. Turn, brown second side.

Makes 6 to 8 individual servings.
SUGGESTED CREPE BATTER: ENTREE I
SUGGESTED CREPE FOLD: FRY FOLD

CREAM CHEESE AND OLIVE ROLL-UPS

2 3-ounce packages (170 g)
    cream cheese
4 tablespoons (60 ml) milk

3/4 cup (180 ml) finely chopped
    pimiento-stuffed olives

8 crepes

Let cream cheese stand at room temperature. Add milk gradually, stirring with fork until cheese is spreading consistency. Lay crepe flat, spread surface with cream cheese. Sprinkle with olives, and roll. Refrigerate and cut into bite-size pieces. Garnish with pimiento, or add dash of paprika for color.

Makes 32 to 40 appetizers.

SUGGESTED CREPE BATTER: ENTREE II

SUGGESTED CREPE FOLD: SPIRAL ROLL

CREPES OYSTERS ROCKEFELLER

2 cups (480 ml) Medium White Sauce
2 8-ounce cans (455 g)
    oysters, drained
3 tablespoons (45 ml) butter
    or margarine
2 tablespoons (30 ml) finely
    chopped onion
2 tablespoons (30 ml) finely
    chopped celery
2 tablespoons (30 ml) finely
    chopped parsley

10-ounce package (285 g) chopped
    spinach, thawed
1/2 teaspoon (2.5 ml)
    Worcestershire
6 drops bottled hot pepper sauce
1/4 teaspoon (1.5 ml) salt
Dash nutmeg
1/4 cup (60 ml) grated
    Parmesan cheese

8 crepes

Prepare Medium White Sauce. Cut oysters into bite-size pieces. Saute oysters in electric frypan in 2 tablespoons butter or margarine until edges curl. Remove from frypan. Saute onion, celery and parsley in remaining butter or margarine. Thoroughly drain spinach, add to frypan. Add egg to Medium White Sauce. Stir 1 cup sauce, seasonings and oysters into vegetables. Spoon onto crepes, fold, and place in greased baking dish. Pour remaining sauce over crepes and sprinkle with Parmesan cheese. Bake at 375° F. (190° C.) for 15 minutes or until hot.

Makes 8 individual servings.

SUGGESTED CREPE BATTER: ENTREE II

SUGGESTED CREPE FOLD: TRADITIONAL

CRISPY CHEESE CREPES

1/2 cup (120 ml)
   grated Swiss cheese
1/2 cup (120 ml)
   cottage cheese
2 tablespoons (30 ml) butter
   or margarine

1 small clove garlic, crushed
Paprika
1-2 drops bottled hot pepper sauce
2 tablespoons (30 ml) dry vermouth
   or dry white wine
1 egg, slightly beaten

8 crepes

Combine Swiss cheese, cottage cheese and butter with garlic, dash of paprika, hot pepper sauce and wine in top of double boiler. Stir constantly over slowly boiling water until cheeses are melted into a smooth mixture (about 5 minutes). Remove from heat and spoon mixture onto crepes. Fold for frying. Dip crepes into beaten egg. Fry in 1 inch of oil at 375° F. (190°C.) until browned on both sides. Drain on paper towels and serve immediately. Garnish with small cherry tomatoes or thinly sliced tomato wedges.

Makes 8 individual servings.
SUGGESTED CREPE BATTER: ENTREE II
SUGGESTED CREPE FOLD: SPIRAL FOLD

DIP CHIPS AND CAVIAR

6 cooked crepes (Entree II)
Melted butter
Dried dill weed

1 small jar red caviar
1 pint sour cream
1 lemon

Brush crepes with butter, then sprinkle with dill. Cut each crepe like a pie into 12 to 16 wedges. Place on cookie sheet and bake in 325°F. (163°C.) oven for 8 minutes, or until crispy. Mix caviar into sour cream. Serve dip surrounded by chips and garnished with thin lemon wedges.

Makes 72 to 96 dip chips.

FRIED SPINACH HORS D'OEUVRE

10-ounce package (285 g) frozen
  chopped spinach
2 tablespoons (30 ml) finely
  chopped onion
1 clove garlic, crushed

1 tablespoon (15 ml) butter
  or margarine
1 egg slightly beaten
1/4 cup (60 ml) pine nuts
2 tablespoons (30 ml) grated
  Parmesan cheese

8 crepes

Cook spinach according to package directions. Drain. Saute onion and garlic in butter. Gradually add spinach, egg, pine nuts and cheese. Spoon onto crepes. Remove from heat and fold for frying. Let crepes stand, uncovered, 30 minutes, to dry slightly . Melt butter in electric frypan. Fry until brown on both sides. Serve with plain yogurt as a sauce, and garnish with a cherry tomato.

    Makes 8 individual servings.
    SUGGESTED CREPE BATTER: ENTREE I
    SUGGESTED CREPE FOLD: FRY FOLD

GUACAMOLE APPETIZERS

2 medium avocados
3 tablespoons (45 ml) lime juice
1 tablespoon (15 ml) onion, minced

Salt and pepper to taste
Dash of Tabasco sauce
Shredded lettuce

8 crepes

Peel and pit avocados. Mash with fork and add lime juice, onion, salt, pepper and Tabasco sauce. Spread mixture on crepes; top with shredded lettuce. Fold. Garnish with cherry tomatoes.

    Makes 8 individual servings.
    SUGGESTED CREPE BATTER: ENTREE II
    SUGGESTED CREPE FOLD: TRADITIONAL

HAM CREPES MEXICANA

4-1/2 ounce can (130 g)
  devled ham
3 tablespoons (45 ml) tomato
  sauce or catsup

2 tablespoons (30 ml) finely
  chopped onion
2 tablespoons (30 ml) finely chopped
  green pepper
1/2-3/4 teaspoons (2.5-3.5 ml)
  chili powder

8 crepes

Combine ingredients. Spoon onto crepes and fold for frying. Let crepes stand covered, 30 minutes to dry slightly. Fry filled crepes in butter until brown on both sides. Serve whole, hot.

    Makes 8 individual servings.
    SUGGESTED CREPE BATTER: CORNMEAL
    SUGGESTED CREPE FOLD: FRY FOLD

HOT CHICKEN CREPES

1-1/2 cups (360 ml) minced
    cooked chicken
1 tablespoon (15 ml) finely
    chopped scallion
1 teaspoon (5 ml)
    prepared mustard

1/2 teaspoon (2.5 ml) paprika
2 tablespoons (30 ml) dry sherry
1/4 cup (60 ml)
    cracker crumbs
1/2 cup (120 ml) mayonnaise
Dash Worcestershire

8 crepes

Combine chicken, scallion, mustard, Worcestershire, paprika, sherry and cracker crumbs. Add mayonnaise and mix. Spoon about 2 tablespoons filling onto each crepe. Fold for frying and refrigerate to dry crepes slightly. Melt butter in electric frypan. Fry filled crepes until brown on both sides. Garnish with spiced apple rings.

Makes 8 individual servings.
SUGGESTED CREPE BATTER: ENTREE II
SUGGESTED CREPE FOLD: FRY FOLD

LIEDERKRANZ TRIANGLES

4-ounce package (115 ml)
    Liederkranz cheese,
    room temperature
1 tablespoon (15 ml) butter
    or margarine

3 tablespoons (45 ml) finely
    chopped scallion
1 tablespoon (15 ml) finely chopped
    green pepper
Dash of hot pepper sauce
Salt and pepper

8 crepes

Mash cheese with fork, add butter and mix well. Stir in remaining ingredients. Season to taste with salt and pepper. Spoon onto crepes and fold. Garnish with green pepper rings and small pickled onions.

Nakes 8 individual servings.
SUGGESTED CREPE BATTER: WHOLE WHEAT
SUGGESTED CREPE FOLD: TRIANGLE

LOTS OF "LOX" ROLL-UPS

2 3-ounce packages (170 g) cream
    cheese, softened
4 tablespoons (60 ml) milk

8 slices "lox" (smoked salmon),
    very thin
Onion wedges
Cherry tomatoes

8 crepes

Mix cream cheese with milk to a spreading consistency. Lay crepes flat and spread cheese over surface. Place one slice of salmon on each crepe and shape into spiral roll. Refrigerate. Before serving, slice each filled crepe on the diagonal into 4 or 5 bite-size pieces. Garnish with skewers of cherry tomatoes and onion wedges.

Makes 20 to 40 appetizers.
SUGGESTED CREPE BATTER: ENTREE II
SUGGESTED CREPE FOLD: SPIRAL ROLL

MUSHROOM HORS D'OEUVRE

1/2 pound (225 g) sliced bacon
1 pound (455 g) mushrooms,
   thinly sliced
2 tablespoons (30 ml) finely
   chopped onion
1/2 teaspoon (2.5 ml) thyme

Salt and pepper
Medium White Sauce
1/4 teaspoon (1.5 ml) paprika
2 tablespoons (30 ml) dry
   white wine
2 teaspoons (10 ml) lemon juice

8 crepes

Fry bacon, drain on paper towels. Reserve 2 tablespoons dripping. Saute mushrooms and onion in drippings. Remove from heat and crumble bacon into mushrooms. Season with thyme, salt and pepper. Prepare White Sauce, add paprika, wine and lemon juice. Add mushroom mixture to seasoned White Sauce, mix well. Spoon hot mushroom filling into crepes. Fold each crepe. Garnish with paper-thin slices of lemon.

Makes 8 individual servings.
SUGGESTED CREPE BATTER: ENTREE II
SUGGESTED CREPE FOLD: TRADITIONAL

NUTTY BLUE CHEESE ROLL-UPS

8 ounces (225 g) blue cheese
4 tablespoons (60 ml) milk

1/2 cup (120 ml) walnuts, chopped

8 crepes

Let blue cheese soften at room temperature. Add milk gradually, stirring with fork until cheese is spreading consistency. Lay crepe flat, spread surface with cream cheese. Sprinkle with nuts. Fold. Chill. To serve, cut into bite-size pieces, 4 or 5 to each crepe. Garnish with thin slices of apple.

Makes 32 to 40 pieces.
SUGGESTED CREPE BATTER: NUTTY
SUGGESTED CREPE FOLD: SPIRAL

RUSSIAN BLINI

4 ounces (115 g) sour cream
Black or lumpfish caviar

Sieved hard-cooked egg yolk

8 crepes

Into each crepe spoon 1 tablespoon sour cream, 1/2 teaspoon caviar and egg yolk. Fold as for frying. Garnish with thin slices of lemon.

Makes 8 individual servings.
SUGGESTED CREPE BATTER: WHOLE WHEAT
SUGGESTED CREPE FOLD: FRY FOLD

Enjoy a taste of authentic Scandinavian cuisine with the aid
of the Sunbeam M'sieur Crepe Crepemaker.
Left: Swedish Meatball Crepe
Right: Swedish pancakes

Wake up to sunshine with a hearty country-style breakfast of crepes
made with the Sunbeam M'sieur Crepe Crepemaker.
Upper left: Spanish Brunch Crepe
Lower left: Fresh Fruit with Sour Cream Crepe
Right: Pigs in a Blanket Crepe

Ideal for luncheons or dinner parties, crepes made with the
Sunbeam M'sieur Crepe Crepemaker help set the mood for fine dining.
Upper: Speedy Spinach Crepe
Middle: Ham A la King Crepe
Lower: Garden Greens Crepe

Add elegance to everyday entrees, vegetables, and desserts with thin,
delicious crepes made with the Sunbeam M'sieur Crepe Crepemaker.
Top with a tasty sauce or topping for the finishing touch.
Upper left: Chocolate Velvet Dessert Crepe
Middle: Broccoli with Cheese Sauce Crepe
Lower: Denver Brunch Crepe

SAGANAKI (GREEK FOOD FOR THE GODS)

1 tablespoon (15 ml) butter
1 teaspoon (5 ml) flour
1 egg

1 pound (455 g) Kasseri cheese
Brandy
1 whole lemon

8 crepes

Place crepe pan in frypan position. Set heat control knob at high position of frying range. Melt butter in frypan. Mix flour and egg together. Cut cheese into logs approximately 4 inches long and 1 inch thick. Dip cheese into egg mixture. Place in frypan and fry until light brown and just beginning to melt, turning once. Remove cheese from frypan and place on crepe. Pour 1 ounce brandy on each crepe and flame. Squeeze lemon over cheese. When flame burns down, wrap crepe and serve immediately. Garnish with paper-thin lemon slices sprinkled with finely chopped parsley.

Makes 8 individual servings.
SUGGESTED CREPE BATTER: ENTREE I
SUGGSTED CREPE FOLD: SPIRAL OR TRADITIONAL

SHRIMP RISSOLES

1 small onion, finely chopped
2 tablespoons (30 ml) olive oil
1/2 pound (225 g) shrimp,
    shelled, deveined and
    chopped fine
2 tablespoons (30 ml) chopped
    parsley

2 eggs, separated
3 tablespoons (45 ml) flour
3/4 teaspoon (3.5 ml) salt
Dash pepper
1 teaspoon (5 ml) lemon juice
Oil for frying

8 crepes

In frypan, saute onion in hot olive oil until tender. Add shrimp and cook until opaque. Remove from heat. Combine parsley, egg yolks, flour, salt, pepper and lemon juice. Gradually beat egg whites until stiff and fold into shrimp mixture. Spoon mixture onto crepe and fold for frying. Fry two or three at a time in inch of oil at 375°F. (190°C.) for 3-4 minutes or until browned. Turn once. Garnish with parsley.

Makes 8 individual servings.
SUGGESTED CREPE BATTER: ENTREE II
SUGGESTED CREPE FOLD: FRY FOLD

SHRIMP TOAST

3/4 cup (180 ml) raw minced
    shrimp
1 egg, beaten
3 tablespoons (45 ml) finely
    chopped scallion

1/2 teaspoon (2.5 ml) cornstarch
1/4 teaspoon (1.5 ml) minced
    fresh ginger
1/4 teaspoon (1.5 ml) salt
Dash pepper
Oil for frying

3 crepes
    Combine shrimp, egg, scallion, cornstarch, ginger, salt and pepper in bowl. Cut crepes into quarters. Spoon shrimp mixture onto flat crepe sections. Using a wide spatula or pancake turner, lower crepe sections into hot oil (375°F.—190°C.) in frypan. Fry until brown, turn, and continue to fry until crisp. Drain on paper towels. Serve hot as appetizers.
    Makes 12 appetizers.
SUGGESTED CREPE BATTER: ENTREE II
SUGGESTED CREPE FOLD: FRY FOLD

SNACK STACK

2 tablespoons (30 ml) milk
8-ounce package (225 g) cream
    cheese, softened
1 cup (240 ml) olives stuffed with
    pimiento, chopped

3 4-1/2-ounce cans (375 g)
    deviled ham
3/4 cup (180 ml) mayonnaise
1 tablespoon (15 ml) lemon juice
1 tablespoon (15 ml) white
    horseradish

24 crepes
    In a medium bowl, mix milk with cream cheese to thin. Stir in olives. In a second bowl, mix deviled ham with mayonnaise, lemon juice and horseradish until smooth. Put one crepe on serving plate and spread thin layer of ham mixture. Top with another crepe and spread with a thin layer of cheese mixture. Repeat until all crepes have been stacked. Chill stack. Before serving, spoon dollop of mayonnaise in center of top crepe; sprinkle with capers. Garnish with cherry tomatoes and parsley around outer edge of top crepe and base of stack. Cut into thin wedges to serve.
    Makes 24 servings.
SUGGESTED CREPE BATTER: RYE
SUGGESTED CREPE FOLD: STACK

SPICY INDIAN CREPES

1 tablespoon (15 ml) oil
1/2 pound (225 ml) ground beef
2 tablespoons (30 ml) minced
  onion
1/2 teaspoon (2.5 ml) ground
  cumin
1/4 teaspoon (1.5 ml) ground
  coriander

1/2 teaspoon (2.5 ml) chili powder
1/8 teaspoon (1 ml) salt
Dash pepper
2 tablespoons (30 ml) butter
  or margarine
Yogurt Dip

8 crepes

Brown beef, onion and seasonings in hot oil. Drain grease. Spoon filling into
each crepe. Fold for frying. Fry filled crepes in butter or margarine until brown and
crisp on both sides. Serve with Yogurt Dip.

Makes 8 individual servings.
SUGGESTED CREPE BATTER: WHOLE WHEAT
SUGGESTED CREPE FOLD: FRY FOLD

Yogurt Dip: Combine 1 cup (240 ml) plain yogurt, 1 clove crushed garlic, 3
tablespoons (45 ml) catsup and 2-3 drops hot pepper sauce.

SWEET SPICE APPETIZER

16-ounce jar (455 g) prepared
  mustard
10-ounce jar (285 g) currant jelly

6 frankfurters; sliced in
  bite-size pieces
10-ounce can (285 g) pineapple
  chunks
1 cup (240 ml) ham cubes

6 to 8 crepes

In saucepan, combine mustard and currant jelly. Cut crepes in quarters and
wrap frankfurters, pineapple chunks or ham cube in crepe wrapper. Secure with
toothpick. Dip in sweet spice sauce.

Makes 24 to 32 pieces.
SUGGESTED CREPE BATTER: ENTREE II

1 pound (455 g) ground beef
2 tablespoons (30 ml)
   chopped onions
1 teaspoon (5 ml) garlic salt
1 teaspoon (5 ml) cumin
2 teaspoons (10 ml) chili powder

1/2 teaspoon (2.5 ml) crushed
   red pepper
Grated cheese
Shredded lettuce
Sliced ripe olives

8 crepes

Brown ground beef and onions in electric frypan. Drain grease. Add seasonings and simmer. Spoon mixture onto crepe and fold. Top with taco sauce. Garnish with grated cheese, shredded lettuce and sliced ripe olives.

Makes 8 individual servings.

SUGGESTED CREPE BATTER: CORNMEAL
SUGGESTED CREPE FOLD: TRIANGLE

MEAT

Bedeviled Ham Crepes
Beef and Vegetable Crepes
Beef Bourguignon Crepes
Beef Enchiladas
Beef Goulash
California Casserole Crepes
Chili Crepes
Chipped Beef Crepes
Corned Beef with Mustard
Cornmeal Franks
Crepes Ragout
Danish Ham Rolls
Easy Beef 'N' Spinach Crepes
Eggplant and Sausage Crepes
Grilled Ham and Cheese
Ham a la King
Ham-Asparagus Rolls
Ham and Broccoli Crepes
Ham 'N' Onion Crepes

Ham and Squash Crepes
Ham and Swiss Sandwich Crepes
Heavenly Hamburger Crepes
Hot Fruit Salad
    and Ham Luncheon Crepes
Hurry-Up Tostados
Lamb Kabob Crepes
Reuben Crepes
Sausage Pepper Crepes
Sloppy Joe Crepes
Spicy Beef and Pepper Crepes
Spicy Beef and Zucchini Crepes
Spicy Kraut and Frank Crepes
Steak Crepes Sublime
Steak Salad Crepes
Steak Surprise
Veal Curry Crepes
Veal Scallopine Cariofo

MAKE THE MOST OF A MEAL ... SERVE CREPES

Crepes have a certain magic about them. Take the most ordinary of fillings, fold in a crepe, and the combination is transformed into an elegant gourmet dish. Quite a trick when you realize that the crepe itself had the humblest of origins. Made from simple country ingredients, these thin pancakes were the food of peasants everywhere. How then did crepes become a princely food? Here's the marvelous magical "true" story about the transformation.

One fine summer day in the year 1490, Anne, the thirteen-year-old daughter of Francois de Bretagne, soon to be Queen of France, set out riding with a group from her father's estate. The day changed and in the forest they were drenched by a downpour so violent that it forced them to take refuge in a woodsman's hut. One of Anne's pages, Pierre, who would one day be Lord of Kerdevot, asked the beautiful daughter of the woodsman, whose name was also Anne, to prepare something for the hungry group to eat. Anne, who made the flat peasant pancakes from black wheat flour each day, labored over the open hearth to prepare a meal fine enough for the high-born company, filling the pancakes with whatever morsels were available. Young Pierre fell in love with her beauty and her baking.

A year later Pierre asked the young Queen Anne for permission to marry the woodsman's daughter who had given them shelter and food that stormy summer day. So it happened that Anne of the Crepes became the Countess de Kergalen.

Yves de Kerdevot, Anne's son, feeling his mother's cooking was fine enough for royalty, introduced the once humble pancake to the court of King Francis. That's how, in a land where food rules supreme, the peasant crepe became one of France's most famous creations.

So bring a little magic into your own kitchen. Be as inventive as Anne, the woodsman's daughter, and people will consider you a "royal" cook.

Meat Crepes

Consider a crepe a "magic horn of plenty" into which you put little and from which you receive much. Just ounces of chicken, veal, lamb, pork, hamburger or sausage can make a dinner for four, six or eight.

Catering to hearty American appetites, we have, in most cases, suggested that the crepe be well filled, though a lighter amount of filling is traditional. So if you find yourself with an extra guest for dinner, or light on meat ... *stretch* with confidence.

For example, say you have one hot dog and two hungry youngsters. Slice the hot dog; warm with a small can of beans; divide in half and wrap in crepes; serve with mustard pickle or relish, and you've made lunch for two.

Leftovers, too, take on a whole new royal character when you mix and match meats and vegetables. Try the fillings in the next pages, but be inventive too. You'll find that crepes can transform any meal into an exciting one.

BEDEVILED HAM CREPES

2 cups (480 ml) cooked ham, chopped fine
1 tablespoon (15 ml) green pepper, chopped fine
1 tablespoon (15 ml) green onion, chopped fine

2 hard-cooked eggs, minced
1 cup (240 ml) sour cream
2 tablespoons (30 ml) whole-grain mustard
1/4 teaspoon (1.5 ml) cayenne
Salt and pepper to taste
Dash of Worcestershire sauce

8 crepes

In medium-size bowl, mix ham, green pepper, onion and eggs together. Mix sour cream with mustard, cayenne, salt and pepper and Worcestershire sauce. Add to ham mixture. Spoon mixture onto crepes. Fold. Dot crepes with butter. Bake in greased baking dish in preheated 375° F. (190°C.) oven for 15 to 20 minutes. Garnish with green pickle relish.

Makes 4 servings of 2 crepes each.
SUGGESTED CREPE BATTER: ENTREE I
SUGGESTED CREPE FOLD: SPIRAL

BEEF AND VEGETABLE CREPES

1 pound (455 g) ground beef
1/2 teaspoon (2.5 ml) salt
1/8 teaspoon (1 ml) pepper
2 tablespoons (30 ml) oil
1/2 pound (225 g) mushrooms, coarsely chopped
1 small onion, finely chopped
1 carrot, finely diced

1/2 cup (120 ml) finely diced celery
2 tablespoons (30 ml) finely chopped green pepper
1 clove garlic, minced
10-1/2-ounce can (300 g) beef, mushroom or brown gravy

8 crepes

Sprinkle beef with salt and pepper, brown in oil in electric frypan. Remove from frypan and discard all but about 2 tablespoons grease. Saute vegetables and garlic in drippings until just tender. Add meat and enough gravy to bind ingredients together, about 1/3 can. Spoon onto crepes, fold and place over crepes. Bake at 350°F (177° C.) for 10 minutes. Garnish with green pepper rings.

Makes 8 individual crepes.
SUGGESTED CREPE BATTER: ENTREE I
SUGGESTED CREPE FOLD: TRADITIONAL

BEEF BOURGUIGNON CREPES

2 slices bacon
1-1/2 pounds (680 g) lean stewing beef,
    cut into 1-inch cubes
1 medium onion, minced
3/4 teaspoon (3.5 ml) salt
Dash pepper
1 tablespoon (15 ml) flour

1-1/2 cups (360 ml) red
    Burgundy wine
1 cup (240 ml) beef stock
1 clove garlic, mashed
1/2 teaspoon (2.5 ml) thyme
1 small bay leaf
1 cup (240 ml) Mushroom Sauce

8 crepes

Fry bacon in Dutch oven; remove. Brown meat and onion in drippings. Add salt, pepper and flour; stir over low heat until flour is browned. Add wine, beef stock and seasongs; cover and simmer until tender, about 2 hours. If mixture is too thin, thicken with 1 tablespoon cornstarch and 1/4 cup water. Cook until thick gravy consistency. Spoon mixture onto crepes. Fold and place in greased baking dish. Pour Mushroom Sauce over crepes and bake at 350° F. (177° C.) for 10 minutes, or until hot and bubbly. Garnish with carrot curls.

Makes 4 servings of 2 crepes each.
SUGGESTED CREPE BATTER: ENTREE II
SUGGESTED CREPE FOLD: TRADITIONAL

BEEF ENCHILADAS

1 pound (455 g) ground beef
1 medium onion, chopped
1 clove garlic, crushed
10-ounce can (285 g) enchilada sauce
Few grains crushed red
    pepper flakes

1 cup (240 ml) grated
    Cheddar cheese
1/4 cup (60 ml) sliced
    ripe olives
2 cups (480 ml) shredded lettuce

8 crepes

Brown beef, onion and garlic. Drain grease. Add enchilada sauce and red pepper flakes, simmer 20 minutes. Spoon meat and Cheddar cheese onto each crepe. Fold and place in greased baking dish. Spoon remaining sauce over crepes. Bake at 350° F. (177° C.) for 15 minutes, or until cheese melts. Serve topped with sliced ripe olives, lettuce and crumbled Mexican or Cheddar cheese.

Makes 4 servings of 2 crepes each.
SUGGESTED CREPE BATTER: CORNMEAL
SUGGESTED CREPE FOLD: TRADITIONAL

BEEF GOULASH

1 pound (455 g) lean beef stew meat,
    cut into 1/2-inch cubes
1/4 cup (60 ml) flour
1/4 teaspoon (1.5 ml) salt
1 cup (240 ml) chopped onions
3 tablespoons (45 ml) butter
    or margarine

2 tablespoons (30 ml) catsup
2 teaspoons (10 ml) paprika
1/2 teaspoon (2.5 ml) thyme leaves
1 clove garlic, minced
1-1/2 cups (360 ml) beef
    bouillon

8 crepes

Toss meat with flour and salt. Brown meat and onions in butter. Stir in catsup, paprika, thyme and garlic. Add bouillon and stir over medium heat until thickened. Simmer, covered, about 1-1/2 hours, or until meat is tender. Stir occasionally, adding water if necessary to prevent sticking. Spoon onto crepes. Fold and serve immediately. Garnish with carrot curls and parsley.

Makes 4 servings of 2 crepes each.
SUGGESTED CREPE BATTER: ENTREE I
SUGGESTED CREPE FOLD: TRADITIONAL

CALIFORNIA CASSEROLE CREPES

1 pound (455 g) ground beef
1/2 teaspoon (2.5 ml) salt
1/4 teaspoon (1.5 ml) garlic powder
Dash pepper
1 small onion, chopped

1 can cream of mushroom
    or cream of celery soup,
    undiluted
1/2 cup (120 ml) milk
10-ounce package (285 g) frozen
    mixed vegetables

8 crepes

Sprinkle beef with seasonings. Brown beef and onion in skillet. Drain grease. Stir in one-half can soup, milk and vegetables. Simmer, covered, until vegetables are tender. Spoon onto crepes and fold. Thin remaining soup with 1 to 2 tablespoons milk and serve over crepes. Sprinkle with paprika and garnish with parsley.

Makes 4 servings of two crepes each.
SUGGESTED CREPE BATTER: ENTREE I
SUGGESTED CREPE FOLD: TRADITIONAL

CHILI CREPES

1 pound (455 g) ground beef	1 teaspoon (5 ml) ground cumin
1 clove garlic, minced	Crushed red pepper flakes
2 medium onions, chopped	1 teaspoon (5 ml) salt
1 tablespoon (15 ml) oil	1/2 teaspoon (2.5 ml) basil
1-pound can (455 g) tomatoes, packed in puree	1 small bay leaf
2 cups water	16-ounce can (455 g) red kidney beans, drained
2 tablespoons (30 ml) chili powder	1 green pepper, chopped

12 crepes

Brown beef, garlic and onions in oil. Drain grease. Add tomatoes, water and seasonings. Simmer 2 hours, stirring occasionally. Add drained kidney beans and green pepper, simmer 30 minutes, or until thick. Spoon onto crepes, fold and serve immediately. Garnish with spoonful of sour cream sprinkled with chives.

Makes 6 servings of 2 crepes each.
SUGGESTED CREPE BATTER: CORNMEAL
SUGGESTED CREPE FOLD: TRADITIONAL

CHIPPED BEEF CREPES

Medium White Sauce, prepared without salt	Dash white pepper
1/4 teaspoon (1.5 ml) salt	1-1/2 cups (360 ml) diced beef

8 crepes

Prepare Medium White Sauce. Stir in spices and dried beef. Spoon onto warm crepes and fold. Serve immediately. Garnish with parsley.

Makes 4 servings of 2 crepes each.
SUGGESTED CREPE BATTER: NUTTY CREPE
SUGGESTED CREPE FOLD: TRADITIONAL

CORNED BEEF WITH MUSTARD

1 cup (240 ml) Medium White Sauce	1-1/2 cups (360 ml) finely chopped lean corned beef or pastrami
2 to 3 teaspoons (10-15 ml) prepared mustard with horseradish	
1/2 teaspoon (2.5 ml) cider vinegar	

8 crepes

Prepare White Sauce. Stir mustard and vinegar into sauce and mix well. Add corned beef. Heat thoroughly. Spoon onto crepes, and fold. Serve with pickle chips.

Makes 4 servings of 2 crepes each.
SUGGESTED CREPE BATTER: RYE
SUGGESTED CREPE FOLD: TRADITIONAL

CORNMEAL FRANKS

4 frankfurters

4 slices processed
American cheese

8 crepes

Cut frankfurters in half across width. Cut 2/3 lengthwise through each half. Place 1/2 slice of cheese in cut. Place on crepe. Fold. Fry in 1 inch of oil on both sides until golden brown. Garnish with mustard pickle.

Makes 4 servings of 2 crepes each.
SUGGESTED CREPE BATTER: CORNMEAL
SUGGESTED CREPE FOLD: FRY

CREPES RAGOUT

1-1/2 pounds (680 g) veal stew
    meat, cut in 1-inch cubes
2 tablespoons (30 ml) butter
    or margarine
1 medium onion, sliced
2 tablespoons (30 ml) flour
1/2 cup (120 ml) dry white
    wine or vermouth
1/2 cup (120 ml) beef bouillon

1 clove garlic, minced
1 bay leaf
1/2 teaspoon (2.5 ml) thyme
1/2 stalk celery
2 tablespoons (30 ml) chopped parsley
1 tablespoon (15 ml) catsup
3/4 teaspoon (3.5 ml) salt
Dash pepper

8 crepes

Brown veal in butter. Add onion and stir occasionally until tender. Remove from heat and stir in flour. Cook over low heat 1-2 minutes, stirring to prevent burning. Add remaining ingredients and simmer 45 minutes, or until meat is tender and gravy is thick. Remove celery. Spoon filling onto crepes and fold. Serve immediately, garnished with carrot curls.

Makes 4 servings of 2 crepes each.
SUGGESTED CREPE BATTER: ENTREE II
SUGGESTED CREPE FOLD: TRADITIONAL

DANISH HAM ROLLS

8 leeks
8 slices Danish ham
Prepared mustard
1 cup (240 ml) Medium
   White Sauce

4 ounces Samsoe cheese,
   grated
1 tablespoon (15 ml) butter
   or margarine
2 tablespoons (30 ml) bread crumbs
Paprika

8 crepes

Cut off top of leeks, leaving about 3-inch lengths at the bottom. Simmer in a small amount of boiling salted water until tender, about 10 minutes. Spread crepes lightly with mustard. Place ham slice and one leek on each crepe. Roll up and place in greased baking dish. Prepare White Sauce. Combine sauce with half the cheese, and pour over crepes. Melt butter and stir bread crumbs in butter to coat. Sprinkle remaining cheese, the bread crumbs and paprika over crepes. Bake at 350° F. (177°C.) about 10 minutes to heat, then broil to brown. Serve with mustard pickles.

Makes 4 servings of 2 crepes each.
SUGGESTED CREPE BATTER: ENTREE I
SUGGESTED CREPE FOLD: SPIRAL ROLL

EASY BEEF 'N' SPINACH CREPES

1/2 pound (225 g) ground beef
   or veal
1 small onion, chopped
1 tablespoon (15 ml) oil
10-ounce package (285 g) frozen
   chopped spinach,
   thawed
3/4 cup (180 ml) soft
   bread crumbs

2 tablespoons (30 ml) grated
   Parmesan cheese
2 eggs, beaten
3/4 teaspoon (3.5 ml) salt
1/4 teaspoon (1.5 ml) garlic salt
Dash pepper
1 cup (240 ml) Marinara Sauce
   (canned or from
   Marina Sauce recipe)

8 crepes

Brown beef and onion in oil. Drain grease. Thoroughly drain spinach, add to meat. Add remaining ingredients and Marinara Sauce, mix well. Spoon onto crepes, fold, and place in greased baking dish. Pour 3/4 cup marinara sauce over top, sprinkle with additional Parmesan cheese, if desired, and bake at 350° F. (177° C.) for 20-30 minutes, or until hot. Garnish with thin slices of hard-boiled egg brushed with paprika.

Makes 4 servings of 2 crepes each.
SUGGESTED CREPE BATTER: ENTREE I
SUGGESTED CREPE FOLD: TRADITIONAL

EGGPLANT AND SAUSAGE CREPES

1 medium eggplant
2 teaspoons (10 ml) salt
2 tablespoons (10 ml) olive oil
1/2 pound (225 g) pork sausage
1 medium onion, chopped
1 clove garlic, crushed
1 large tomato, peeled,
    seeded and chopped

3 tablespoons (45 ml) dry white wine
1/2 teaspoon (2.5 ml) salt
Dash pepper
Dash cinnamon
1/2 cup (120 ml) cooked
    white rice
1 egg, slightly beaten
Parmesan cheese

8 crepes

Peel eggplant, cut into 1/2-inch cubes. Sprinkle with salt and let stand 15 minutes. Rinse and dry on paper towels. In frypan saute eggplant in hot olive oil until tender. Remove from pan. Brown sausage, onion and garlic in same pan, drain off grease. Add tomato, wine, salt, pepper and cinnamon. Cover and simmer until most of liquid has evaporated, about 10 minutes. Add rice, eggplant and egg; mix well. Spoon mixture onto crepes. Fold and place in greased baking dish. Sprinkle with Parmesan cheese and bake at 350° F. (177° C.) for 20 minutes, or until hot. Garnish with parsley.

Makes 4 servings of 2 crepes each.
SUGGESTED CREPE BATTER: ENTREE II
SUGGESTED CREPE FOLD: TRADITIONAL

GRILLED HAM AND CHEESE

1 egg, slightly beaten
1/4 cup (60 ml) milk
1/4 teaspoon (1.5 ml) salt
Dash pepper

8 thin slices ham
8 thin slices Swiss cheese
Butter or margarine
    for frying

8 crepes

Combine egg, milk, salt and pepper in shallow dish. Place crepes on platter with brown side up. Top each with a slice of ham and cheese. Fold, dip in egg mixture, and fry in butter over medium heat until brown. Turn and brown other side. Serve hot, garnished with mustard pickle.

Makes 4 servings of 2 crepes each.
SUGGESTED CREPE BATTER: ENTREE II
SUGGESTED CREPE FOLD: FRY FOLD

HAM A LA KING

10-ounce package (285 g) frozen peas
2 tablespoons (30 ml) margarine
1 cup (240 ml) sliced mushrooms
3 tablespoons (45 ml) chopped
   green onions
1/4 cup (60 ml) diced green pepper

3 hard-cooked eggs
2 cups (480 ml) ham,
   cooked and cubed
1/2 teaspoon (2.5 ml) salt
1/4 teaspoon (1.5 ml) dry mustard

WHITE SAUCE

1/4 cup (60 ml) melted margarine
1/4 cup (60 ml) flour
2 cups (480 ml) milk

1/4 teaspoon (1.5 ml) salt
Dash white pepper

8 crepes

Prepare peas as directed on package. Drain. Melt margarine in frypan. Saute mushrooms, chopped green onions and green pepper until tender. In saucepan, combine flour and melted margarine for white sauce. Cook over medium heat, gradually adding milk. Stir sauteed vegetables, eggs, ham, peas, salt and dry mustard to white sauce and heat thoroughly. Spoon mixture onto crepe. Fold, top with additional mixture and garnish with pimiento.

Makes 4 servings of 2 crepes each.
SUGGESTED CREPE BATTER: ENTREE I
SUGGESTED CREPE FOLD: TRADITIONAL

HAM-ASPARAGUS ROLLS

10-ounce package (285 g) frozen
   asparagus spears

8 thin slices baked ham
Mock Hollandaise Sauce

8 crepes

Cook asparagus according to package directions. Wrap 2-3 spears in each ham slice, place in crepes and roll up. Place in greased baking dish. Bake at 350° F. (177° C.) for 10 minutes, or until hot. Prepare Mock Hollandaise Sauce. Spoon over crepes. Sprinkle with paprika. Serve immediately, garnished with pimiento.

Makes 4 servings of 2 crepes each.
SUGGESTED CREPE BATTER: ENTREE II
SUGGESTED CREPE FOLD: SPIRAL ROLL

HAM AND BROCCOLI CREPES

10-ounce package (285 g) frozen
chopped broccoli
1 small onion, chopped
2-1/2 cups (600 ml) diced,
cooked ham
2 tablespoons (30 ml) butter
or margarine
1/2 cup (120 ml) process cheese spread

1/4 cup (60 ml) milk
10-1/2-ounce can (300 g) cream of
celery soup, undiluted
1/4 teaspoon (1.5 ml) thyme
1/4 teaspoon (1.5 ml) Worcestershire
1 cup (240 ml) packaged quick-
cooking rice, uncooked

8 crepes

Cook broccoli according to package directions until just tender, drain. Saute onion and ham in butter in electric frypan. Combine cheese spread and milk, add to ham. Add broccoli, soup, thyme, Worcestershire and rice to ham. Bring to boil, stirring frequently. Cover and simmer until rice is done and mixture is thick. Spoon onto crepes, fold and serve immediately. Garnish with pimiento strips.

Makes 4 servings, 2 crepes each.
SUGGESTED CREPE BATTER: ENTREE
SUGGESTED CREPE FOLD: TRADITIONAL

HAM 'N' ONION CREPES

9-ounce package (255 g) frozen green
peas and small onions
with cream sauce

1 cup (240 ml) minced ham

8 crepes

Cook frozen vegetables according to package directions. Add ham; heat. Spoon onto crepes and fold. Top with any unused vegetable-and-ham mixture. Garnish with pimiento.

Makes 4 servings of 2 crepes each.
SUGGESTED CREPE BATTER: ENTREE II
SUGGESTED CREPE FOLD: TRADITIONAL

HAM AND SQUASH CREPES

1/2 cup (120 ml) diced pie
   (tart) apples
1 tablespoon (15 ml) butter
   or margarine
1 medium acorn squash,
   cooked and diced

3/4 cup (180 ml) finely
   diced ham
1/4 teaspoon (1.5 ml) dry mustard
Dash pepper

8 crepes

Saute apple in butter until tender. Add remaining ingredients and heat. Spoon onto crepes, fold and serve immediately. Garnish with thinly sliced wedges of red-skinned apples

Makes 4 servings of 2 crepes each.
SUGGESTED CREPE BATTER: ENTREE
SUGGESTED CREPE FOLD: TRADITIONAL

HAM AND SWISS SANDWICH CREPES

4 slices Swiss cheese
4 slices boiled ham or
   8 slices salami

Prepared mustard
4 drained sweet gherkins

4 crepes

Lay Swiss cheese on crepe. Top with ham or salami, spread meat with mustard and place pickle in center. Roll up and serve. Garnish with parsley.

Makes 4 individual servings.
SUGGESTED CREPE BATTER: ENTREE II
SUGGESTED CREPE FOLD: SPIRAL ROLL

HEAVENLY HAMBURGER CREPES

1 pound (455 g) beef chuck,
   ground
1 teaspoon (5 ml) salt
1/8 teaspoon (1 ml) pepper
1 egg
1 medium onion, chopped

10-1/2-ounce can (300 g) cream
   of mushroom soup
1/4 cup (60 ml) milk
3-ounce can (85 g) mushrooms,
   drained

8 crepes

Mix beef, salt, pepper, egg and onion. Shape into 8 very flat meat patties. Cook. Meanwhile, heat mushroom soup, milk and mushrooms. Place meat patty in center of crepe. Pour mushroom mixture over meat. Fold. Pour remaining mushroom mixture over crepes. Sprinkle with paprika and garnish with parsley.

Makes 4 servings of 2 crepes each.
SUGGESTED CREPE BATTER: CORN
SUGGESTED CREPE FOLD: HALF

HOT FRUIT SALAD AND HAM LUNCHEON CREPES

2 cups (480 ml) canned
    fruit salad
2 cups (480 ml) ham, diced

3/4 cup (180 ml) mayonnaise
3 tablespoons (45 ml) lemon juice

8 crepes

Wash and drain fruit salad. Add ham chunks. In small bowl, mix fruit and ham with mayonnaise and lemon juice. Spoon mixture onto crepes. Fold. Place in greased baking pan and warm in preheated oven at 350°F. (177° C.) for about 10 to 15 minutes. Garnish with slices of banana dusted with nutmeg.

Makes 4 servings of 2 crepes each.
SUGGESTED CREPE BATTER: NUTTY
SUGGESTED CREPE FOLD: SPIRAL

HURRY-UP TOSTADOS

1 pound (455 g) ground beef
1 onion, sliced
1 teaspoon (5 ml) garlic salt
1 teaspoon (5 ml) cumin
2 teaspoons (10 ml) chili powder
16-ounce can (455 g) refried
    beans, heated

2 tablespoons (30 ml) water
1/4 pound (115 g) grated
    Cheddar cheese
1/2 head lettuce, shredded
1 tomato, diced
1 small onion, chopped
1 jar taco sauce

8 crepes

Brown meat and onion. Drain grease. Stir in seasonings, simmer 10 minutes. Place crepes on baking sheet without overlapping and bake in preheated 400° F. (218° C.) oven for 4 minutes, or until crepes are crisp. To serve, spread crisp crepes with hot refried beans; spoon meat mixture over top. Sprinkle with cheese. Top with lettuce, tomato, onion and taco sauce.

Makes 4 servings of 2 crepes each.
SUGGESTED CREPE BATTER: CORNMEAL

LAMB KABOB CREPES

1/3 cup (80 ml) lemon juice
3 tablespoons (45 ml) olive oil
1 teaspoon (5 ml) salt
3/4 teaspoon (3.5 ml) ground cumin
1/4 teaspoon (1.5 ml) pepper
1/4 teaspoon (1.5 ml) tumeric

1/4 teaspoon (1.5 ml)
    crushed red pepper flakes
1-3/4 pound (790 g) lean lamb,
    cut into 3/4-inch cubes
1 large onion, thinly sliced
1 cup (240 ml) yogurt
2 tomatoes, diced

8 crepes

Combine lemon juice, olive oil and seasonings in a marinade. Pour one-half marinade over lamb anad remaining half over onion. Chill both for at least 2 hours, stirring occasionally. Place meat on skewers, reserving marinade. Broil or grill 3-4 inches from heat until done, about 12 to 15 minutes. Brush with marinade during cooking. Remove skewers and spoon meat onto crepes. Fold and place on serving platter. Spoon yogurt over crepes. Top with slices of tomato. Drain onions well and serve with crepes.

Makes 4 servings of 2 crepes each.
SUGGESTED CREPE BATTER: ENTREE I
SUGGESTED CREPE FOLD: TRADITIONAL

REUBEN CREPES

1 pound (455 g) lean corned beef,
    thinly sliced
2 8-ounce cans (455 g) sauerkraut

1-1/2 cup (360 ml) Swiss cheese
Prepared horseradish
    mustard

8 crepes

Spoon 3 or 4 tablespoons sauerkraut on each crepe, top with slices of corned beef and sprinkle with cheese. Fold. Place in baking dish and bake at 375° F. (190° C.) until cheese melts. Brush crepes with horseradish mustard. Garnish with dill pickles.

Makes 4 servings of 2 crepes each.
SUGGESTED CREPE BATTER: RYE
SUGGESTED CREPE FOLD: SPIRAL ROLL

SAUSAGE PEPPER CREPES

1-1/2 pound (680 g) pork sausage
1/2 cup (120 ml) chopped
   green pepper
21-ounce jar (595 g) tomato sauce
1/4 pound (115 g) grated sharp
   Cheddar cheese

8 crepes

Brown sausage. Drain grease. Add green pepper. Reserve 1 cup tomato sauce; add remainder to sausage. Simmer 10 minutes. Spoon sausage mixture onto crepes. Sprinkle with cheese, setting aside about 1/3 for topping. Fold crepes and place in baking dish. Pour reserved sauce over crepes and sprinkle with reserved cheese. Bake at 350° F. (177° C.) for 10 to 15 minutes, or until bubbling and cheese is melted. Do not overcook. Garnish with pimiento and anchovies.

Makes 4 servings of 2 crepes each.
SUGGESTED CREPE BATTER: ENTREE I
SUGGESTED CREPE FOLD: TRADITIONAL

SLOPPY JOE CREPES

1 pound (455 g) ground beef
1 medium onion, chopped
1 clove garlic, minced
1 tablespoon (15 ml) oil
Dash pepper
10-1/ ounce can (300 g) chicken gumbo
   or vegetable soup, undiluted
6-ounce can (170 g) tomato paste
1 green onion, chopped

8 crepes

Brown beef, onion and garlic in oil. Drain grease. Add soup, tomato paste, green onion and pepper. Simmer, covered, until thick, about 30 minutes. Spoon onto crepes and fold. Serve with chopped onion and Parmesan cheese.

Makes 4 servings of 2 crepes each.
SUGGESTED CREPE BATTER: ENTREE II
SUGGESTED CREPE FOLD: HALF

SPICY BEEF AND PEPPER CREPES

1 pound (455 g) ground beef
1 clove garlic, minced
1/4 cup (60 ml) diced celery
1/3 cup (80 ml) chopped onion
1/2 cup (120 ml) chopped green pepper
2 tablespoons (30 ml) olive oil
1/2 cup (120 ml) sliced pimiento
   stuffed olives

1/4 cup (60 ml) dark seedless raisins
1 tablespoon (15 ml) capers
1/2 teaspoon (2.5 ml) cumin
   or chili powder
Dash ground allspice
8-ounce can (225 g) tomato sauce
Salt and pepper

8 crepes

In frypan, saute ground beef, garlic, celery, onion and green pepper in olive oil. Drain grease. Stir in olives, raisins, capers, cumin, allspice and 1/3 tomato sauce. Season with salt and pepper. Spoon onto crepes. Fold, and place in baking dish. Pour remaining tomato sauce over crepes and bake in oven at 350° F. (177° C.) until hot. Garnish with skewers of pickled onion and cherry tomato.

Makes 4 servings of 2 crepes each.
SUGGESTED CREPE BATTER: ENTREE I
SUGGESTED CREPE FOLD: TRADITIONAL

SPICY BEEF AND ZUCCHINI CREPES

1 pound (455 g) ground beef
1/2 teaspoon (2.5 ml) salt
2 tablespoons (30 ml) oil
1 medium zucchini, diced
1 small onion, chopped
1 clove garlic, minced

1/2 cup (120 ml) cooked rice
1/4 cup (60 ml) catsup
1/2 teaspoon (2.5 ml) bottled
   hot pepper sauce
1/4 teaspoon (1.5 ml) cayenne pepper
8-ounce can (225 g) tomato sauce

8 crepes

Sprinkle meat with salt; brown in oil. Remove from frypan and drain grease, reserving 2 tablespoons. Saute zucchini, onion and garlic in drippings until tender. Add beef, rice, catsup, hot pepper sauce and 1/8 teaspoon cayenne. Heat, stirring occasionally. Heat tomato sauce, add 1/8 teaspoon cayenne. Spoon meat mixture onto crepes. Fold. Pour tomato sauce over crepes. Garnish with raw zucchini spears dusted with paprika.

Makes 4 servings of 2 crepes each.
SUGGESTED CREPE BATTER: ENTREE I
SUGGESTED CREPE FOLD: TRADITIONAL

SPICY KRAUT AND FRANK CREPES

1 cup (240 ml) sour cream
2 tablespoons (30 ml) spicy
  brown mustard
1 small onion, chopped
Butter or margarine
16-ounce can (455 g) sauerkraut

1/4 cup (60 ml) apple cider
1 medium-size apple,
  diced
1/2 teaspoon (2.5 ml) caraway seed
2 teaspoons (10 ml) brown sugar
8 frankfurters

8 crepes

Combine sour cream and mustard, set aside. In frypan, saute onion in 1 tablespoon butter until crisp-tender. Drain sauerkraut, pressing off most of liquid. Add kraut, apple cider, apple and caraway seed to onion. Add brown sugar to taste. Cover and heat until apples are tender, about 3 minutes. Meanwhile, fry franks in 1 tablespoon butter until brown and hot. Place franks on crepes, top with sauerkraut mixture and fold. Serve immediately with sour cream sauce.

Makes 4 servings, 2 crepes each.
SUGGESTED CREPE BATTER: ENTREE
SUGGESTED CREPE FOLD: TRADITIONAL

STEAK CREPES SUBLIME

3 tablespoons (45 ml) butter
  or margarine
1 pound (455 g) top sirloin, cut
  into thin strips

Salt and pepper to taste
2 teaspoons (10 ml) Worcestershire sauce
8-ounce jar (225 g) chutney
1 pint sour cream

8 crepes

Melt butter in skillet. Add meat and brown quickly. Salt and pepper to taste. Add Worcestershire sauce. Spoon meat and juices onto crepes. Top with 1 or 2 tablespoons full of chutney. Fold. Garnish with dollop of sour cream.

Makes 4 servings of 2 crepes each.
SUGGESTED CREPE BATTER: ENTREE I
SUGGESTED CREPE FOLD: TRADITIONAL

STEAK SALAD CREPES

1-1/2 pound (69) g) steak, about
3/4 inch thick, cut in strips
   about 1 inch long
2 tablespoons (30 ml) butter
   or margarine
2 green peppers, sliced thin
1 large cucumber, sliced
   in thin circles

1/2 cup (120 ml) pimiento
1 cup (240 ml) muenster
   cheese, cubed
2 medium onions, sliced thin
2 cups (420 ml) shredded lettuce
2 tablespoons (30 ml) salad oil
1 teaspoon (5 ml) capers
Salt and pepper to taste

8 crepes

Brown steak in butter. Drain. In large bowl, mix steak, green pepper, cucumber, cheese, pimiento, onions, and lettuce with oil. Add capers, and salt and pepper to taste. Spoon mixture onto crepe. Fold. Garnish with carrot curls.

Makes 4 servings of 2 crepes each.
SUGGESTED CREPE BATTER: WHOLE WHEAT
SUGGESTED CREPE FOLD: HALF

STEAK SURPRISE

3 tablespoons (45 ml) butter
   or margarine
1 pound (455 g) sirloin steak
Salt and pepper to taste

1 cup (240 ml) mayonnaise
1/2 cup (120 ml) sweetened coconut
1 teaspoon (5 ml) lemon juice

8 crepes

Melt butter in frypan, add meat and brown quickly. Salt and pepper to taste, Mix mayonnaise, coconut and lemon juice together. Spoon meat onto crepe. Top with 2 tablespoons of mayonnaise mixture. Fold. Garnish with additional mayonnaise mixture.

Makes 4 servings of 2 crepes each.
SUGGESTED CREPE BATTER: ENTREE I
SUGGESTED CREPE FOLD: TRADITIONAL

VEAL CURRY CREPES

1 teaspoon (5 ml) sugar
2 tablespoons (30 ml) butter
　or margarine
1 small onion, minced
1-1/2 pounds (680 g) lean veal,
　cut into 1/2-inch cubes
1/2 teaspoon (7.5 ml)
　curry powder

1 teaspoon (5 ml) salt
Dash pepper
1/4 teaspoon (1.5 ml) paprika
1/4 teaspoon (1.5 ml) dry mustard
2 tablespoons (30 ml) flour
1 cup (240 ml) water
2 tablespoons (30 ml) sour cream

8 crepes

Heat sugar in frypan until melted and slightly brown. Add butter, onion, veal, curry powder, salt, pepper, paprika and mustard. Saute until veal is browned. Mix flour with 1/4 cup water; stir in remaining water. Gradually add flour mixture to veal, stirring constantly until thickened. Simmer, covered, about 30 minutes, or until veal is tender. Spoon mixture onto crepes. Fold, and top with additional mixture. Garnish with sour cream and dust with paprika.

Makes 8 individual servings
SUGGESTED CREPE BATTER: ENTREE II
SUGGESTED CREPE FOLD: TRADITIONAL

VEAL SCALLOPINE CARIOFO

10-ounce package (285 g) frozen
　artichoke hearts
1 pound (455 g) veal cutlets
3 tablespoons (45 ml) flour
1/4 teaspoon (1.5 ml) salt
Dash pepper
2 tablespoons (30 ml) butter
　or margarine
1/2 pound (225 g) mushrooms, sliced
1 chicken bouillon cube

1/2 cup (120 ml) boiling water
1/4 cup (60 ml) sliced pitted
　black olives
4-ounce jar (115 g) pimiento,
　cut into 1/4-inch strips
4 teaspoons (10 ml) juice
　from canned pimientos
6 tablespoons (90 ml) white wine

8 crepes

Prepare artichoke hearts according to package directions. Cut veal into bite-size pieces. Combine flour, salt and pepper. Toss veal with seasoned flour. Saute in butter until brown. Remove from pan, saute mushrooms in drippings. Combine bouillon cube and water. Add bouillon, veal, olives, pimiento, pimiento juice and wine to mushrooms, Cut artichoke hearts in half and add. Cover and simmer 10 minutes, or until hot and veal is tender. Spoon onto crepes. Fold. Garnish with sliced black olives and pimiento strips.

Makes 4 servings of 2 crepes each.
SUGGESTED CREPE BATTER: ENTREE I
SUGGESTED CREPE FOLD: TRADITIONAL

Note: Recipes for sauces which are listed as ingredients in many of the entree crepes may be found in the Sauce chapter.

POULTRY

Cheesy Chicken Luncheon Crepes
Chicken a la King
Chicken and Ham Delights
Chicken Crepes Florentine
Chicken Crepes Veronique
Chicken Divan
Chicken Italiano Crepes
Cranberry and Turkey Crepes
Elegant Chicken Crepes
Mock Cordon Bleu Crepes
Oriental Chicken Crepes
Paprika Chicken Crepes
Sweet and Pungent Chicken Crepes
Turkey Avocado Crepes
Turkey Crepes in Welsh Rarebit Sauce

POULTRY

Chicken in crepes. It's easy to prepare and sure to please everyone.

Combine chicken with vegetables, fruits, other meats, white sauces, brown sauces and spices to produce innumerable combinations to please the most sophisticated or simple of tastes.

As elegant as they are, chicken crepes are economical when you consider that it takes only 1 or 2 cups of chicken to satisfy the appetites of 6 to 8 hungry diners.

You can always be prepared for unexpected company, too, just by cooking extra whenever you make poultry. Bone the extra meat, cut it in small pieces and freeze it in 1- or 2-cup packages.

Defrost and enjoy chicken crepes whenever you wish.

CHEESY CHICKEN LUNCHEON CREPES

12-ounce carton (340 g) cottage cheese with pineapple
2 cups (480 ml) cooked chicken, cubed

1/2 cup (120 ml) walnuts, chopped
Dash cinnamon

8 crepes

In medium-size bowl, soften cottage cheese by mixing with fork. Add chicken and walnuts. Spoon mixture onto crepes. Fold. Spoon teaspoonful of cheese mixture on top. Add dash of cinnamon. Garnish with green grapes or other fruit.

Makes 4 servings of 2 crepes each.
SUGGESTED CREPE BATTER: NUTTY
SUGGESTED CREPE FOLD: SPIRAL

CHICKEN a la KING

1/4 cup (60 ml) mushrooms, sliced
1 tablespoon (15 ml) minced onions
1/4 cup (60 ml) melted margarine
1/3 cup (80 ml) flour
1 teaspoon (5 ml) salt
1 cup (240 ml) chicken stock
1 cup (240 ml) milk

2 cups (480 ml) chicken, cooked and cubes
2 tablespoons (30 ml) pimiento
1/2 cup (120 ml) frozen peas
1 tablespoon minced onion
1/2 teaspoon (2.5 ml) parsley
1/8 teaspoon (1 ml) white pepper

8 to 10 crepes

Saute mushrooms and onions in frypan. In saucepan, combine margarine, flour and salt. Cook over medium heat, gradually adding chicken stock and milk. Stir constantly until mixture thickens. Add chicken, pimiento, peas, onion, parsley and pepper. Heat thoroughly. Spoon mixture onto crepe. Fold. Garnish with sprig of parsley or pimiento strips.

Makes 4 or 5 servings of 2 crepes each.
SUGGESTED CREPE BATTER: ENTREE II
SUGGESTED CREPE FOLD: TRADITIONAL

CHICKEN AND HAM DELIGHTS

2 chicken breasts, skinned
   and boned
3 tablespoons (45 ml) terriyaki
   or soy sauce
3 tablespoons (45 ml) lemon juice
1 tablespoon (15 ml) peanut oil

1/4 pound (115 g) cooked
   ham, diced
1 cup (240 ml) walnuts or
   almonds, chopped fine
1 cup (240 ml) chicken broth
2 teaspoons (10 ml) cornstarch

8 crepes

Cut uncooked chicken into small pieces. Marinate in terriyaki or soy sauce and lemon juice for 1 hour. Heat peanut oil in frypan over medium heat. Add chicken, stirring rapidly over high heat until chicken is done. Reduce heat, add ham and nuts. Reserve 1 tablespoon of chicken broth; add rest to mixture. Mix cornstarch in reserved broth and add to mixture to thicken. Cook for an additional 3 to 4 minutes. Spoon mixture onto crepes. Fold. Place in greased baking dish and bake at 375° F. (190° C.) for 15 minutes. Garnish with walnut halves or almond slivers.

Makes 4 servings of 2 crepes each.

SUGGESTED CREPE BATTER: ENTREE II

SUGGESTED CREPE FOLD: TRADITIONAL

CHICKEN CREPES FLORENTINE

1 cup (240 ml) chicken
10-ounce package (285 g) chopped
   spinach
1/4 cup (60 ml) bread crumbs
1/4 cup (60 ml) Parmesan
   cheese, grated

1 clove garlic, minced
10-1/2 ounce can (300 ml) condensed
   cream of chicken soup
1/2 cup (120 ml) milk
1 hard-cooked egg, crumbled

8 crepes

Mix chicken, spinach, bread crumbs, cheese, garlic and half the soup. Spoon chicken mixture on crepes. Fold, and place in greased baking dish. Combine remaining soup with milk. Pour over crepes. Heat at 350° F. (177° C.) for 15 to 20 minutes. Garnish with slices of hard-cooked egg and thin rounds of lemon brushed with parsley.

Makes 4 servings of 2 crepes each.

SUGGESTED CREPE BATTER: ENTREE II

SUGGESTED CREPE FOLD: TRADITIONAL

CHICKEN CREPES VERONIQUE

3 tablespoons (45 ml) butter
1/4 cup (60 ml) chopped onion
1/2 pound (225 g) fresh
   mushrooms, sliced
3 tablespoons (45 ml) flour
1 cup (240 ml) chicken stock

1/2 teaspoon (2.5 ml) crushed
   tarragon
1/2 teaspoon (2.5 ml) salt
1/4 teaspoon (1.5 ml) pepper
3 cups (720 ml) cooked chicken,
   cut in julienne strips
1/2 cup (120 ml) white wine
2 cups (480 ml) seedless white grapes

8 crepes

Melt butter in frypan. Add onion and mushrooms and saute until tender. Stir in flour. Add chicken stock, wine, tarragon, salt and pepper. Cook over medium-high heat, stirring constantly, until mixture comes to a boil. Remove from heat. Pour 1/2 of sauce and one cup of grapes over chicken, and mix. Spoon about 8 tablespoons of mixture onto each crepe. Fold. Top with remaining sauce and bake in preheated 375° F. (190° C.) oven 15 to 20 minutes. Garnish with remaining grapes.

Makes 4 servings of 2 crepes each.
SUGGESTED CREPE BATTER: ENTREE I
SUGGESTED CREPE FOLD: TRADITIONAL

CHICKEN DIVAN

1-1/2 cups (360 ml) chicken, cooked,
   skinned and diced
10-ounce can (285 g) condensed
   cream of chicken soup

10-ounce package (285 g) frozen
   broccoli spears,
   cooked and drained
1 cup (240 ml) Cheddar cheese,
   grated

8 crepes

Combine chicken and undiluted chicken soup in saucepan; heat thoroughly. Place broccoli spear on each crepe and cover with chicken mixture. Sprinkle grated cheese on top of chicken mixture. Fold crepe. Place in greased casserole and top with remaining cheese. Bake at 350° F. (177° C.) until cheese melts, approximately 15 minutes. Garnish with broccoli flowers or pimiento.

Makes 4 servings of 2 crepes each.
SUGGESTED CREPE BATTER: ENTREE II
SUGGESTED CREPE FOLD: TRADITIONAL

CHICKEN ITALIANO CREPES

1/4 pound (115 g) mushrooms, sliced
1 large onion, chopped
1 large green pepper, chopped
1 clove garlic, minced
3 tablespoons (45 ml) olive oil
4 cups (960 ml) chicken, cooked
    skinned and diced
8-ounce can (225 g) tomato sauce

1 small bay leaf
1/2 teaspoon (2.5 ml) salt
1/2 teaspoon (2.5 ml) oregano
1/2 teaspoon (2.5 ml) basil
Dash pepper
3 tablespoons (45 ml) dry white wine
1/4 pound (115 g) Mozzarella cheese

8 crepes

In frypan, saute mushrooms, onion, green pepper and garlic in oil. Add chicken, tomato sauce, seasonings and wine. Cover and simmer about 15 to 20 minutes. Spoon mixture onto crepes and fold. Place crepes in greased baking dish. Top crepes with cheese and bake at 375° F. (190° C.) for 20 minutes, or until hot and cheese is lightly browned. Garnish with parsley and thin rings of black olive.

Makes 4 servings of 2 crepes each.
SUGGESTED CREPE BATTER: ENTREE II
SUGGESTED CREPE FOLD: TRADITIONAL

CRANBERRY AND TURKEY CREPES

16-ounce can (455 g) whole
    cranberry sauce
2 tablespoons (30 ml) frozen
    orange juice concentrate

3 cups (720 ml) cooked turkey, cubed
1/2 cup (120 ml) walnuts, chopped
1 teaspoon (5 ml) grated
    lemon peel

8 crepes

Combine cranberry sauce and orange juice concentrate in saucepan, stirring until liquid. Add turkey. Heat. Just before removing, add walnuts and lemon peel. Fill each crepe with about 1/4 cup of mixture. Fold. Garnish with thin orange slices dusted with nutmeg.

Makes 4 servings of 2 crepes each.
SUGGESTED CREPE BATTER: NUTTY
SUGGESTED CREPE FOLD: SPIRAL

ELEGANT CHICKEN CREPES

2 cups (480 ml) Bechamel Sauce
1 cup (240 ml) sliced mushrooms
1 tablespoon (15 ml) butter
    or margarine

2 cups (480 ml) diced chicken
Salt and pepper

8 crepes

Prepare Bechamel Sauce. In frypan, saute mushrooms in butter. Add chicken and 3/4 cup Bechamel Sauce. Season to taste with salt and pepper. Spoon onto crepes, fold and place in greased baking dish. Pour remaining sauce over crepes. Bake at 350° F. (177° C.) for 20 minutes, or until hot. Garnish with wedges of cranberry sauce.

Makes 4 servings of 2 crepes each.
SUGGESTED CREPE BATTER: ENTREE II
SUGGESTED CREPE FOLD: TRADITIONAL

MOCK CORDON BLEU CREPES

4 small whole chicken breasts,
    boned and skinned
Salt and pepper
2 tablespoons (30 ml) butter
    or margarine

8 slices of prosciutto,
    paper thin
1/4 pound (115 g) grated
    Mozzarella cheese

8 crepes

Cut each chicken breast into halves. Trim. Sprinkle with salt and pepper. Fry in butter in frypan set on medium heat. Turn frequently to prevent excessive browning. Place one piece of chicken on crepe, top with thin slice of prosciutto, sprinkle with 1 tablespoon Mozzarella. Fold and place in greased baking dish. Bake at 350° F. (177° C.) for 15 to 20 minutes, or until cheese melts. Garnish with parsley or tiny cherry tomatoes.

Makes 4 servings of 2 crepes each.
SUGGESTED CREPE BATTER: ENTREE II
SUGGESTED CREPE FOLD: TRADITIONAL

ORIENTAL CHICKEN CREPES

2 whole chicken breasts,
   boned and skinned
1 tablespoon (15 ml) cornstarch
2 tablespoons (30 ml) soy sauce
1 package (285 g) frozen snow peas
1 teaspoon (5 ml) cornstarch
1/2 cup (120 ml) chicken broth

2 tablespoons (30 ml) sesame oil
1 small onion, sliced
1/2 cup (120 ml) diagonally
   thin-sliced celery
1/2 cup (120 ml) raw cashews,
   coarsely chopped

8 crepes

Place chicken on tray and freeze until firm enough to cut easily, about 30 minutes. Cut 1/8-inch-thick slices across the width of each breast. Combine 1 tablespoon cornstarch and soy sauce, toss with chicken and let stand 20 minutes. Then, in frypan, saute chicken in hot oil until brown and done. Remove from pan. Rinse snow peas to thaw, cut in half and dry on paper towels. Combine 1 teaspoon cornstarch with chicken broth. Add vegetables to pan. Cook, covered, for 2-3 minutes. Remove lid and stir until done. Add chicken and broth, stirring until thick and hot. Stir in cashews. Spoon onto crepes, fold and serve immediately. Garnish with watercress.

Makes 4 servings of 2 crepes each.
SUGGESTED CREPE BATTER: ENTREE II
SUGGESTED CREPE FOLD: TRADITIONAL

PAPRIKA CHICKEN CREPES

1 medium onion, chopped
1 clove garlic, minced
2 tablespoons (30 ml) butter
   or margarine
1 teaspoon (5 ml) paprika
1/4 teaspoon (1.5 ml) ground cumin
1 cup (240 ml) chicken bouillon

2 chicken breasts,
   (approximately 2 cups — 480 ml),
   skinned and boned
3 tablespoons (45 ml) flour
1/4 cup (60 ml) water
Sour cream

8 crepes

In frypan, saute onion and garlic in butter until lightly browned. Stir in paprika and cumin; saute lightly. Add bouillon and chicken pieces. Simmer, covered, until chicken is tender, about 30 minutes. Remove chicken; set aside to cool Combine flour and water, stirring until smooth. Stir into paprika broth; stir constantly over medium heat until thickened. Set aside 1/2 cup sauce. Dice chicken, add to thickened sauce. Simmer 5 minutes, stirring occasionally. Remove from heat and stir in 2 tablespoons sour cream. Spoon hot mixture onto crepes, fold and place in greased baking dish. Add 2 teaspoons sour cream to the 1/2 cup reserved sauce, and spoon over crepes. Bake at 350° F. (177° C.) for 10-20 minutes, or until bubbling. Garnish with parsley.

Makes 4 servings of 2 crepes each.
SUGGESTED CREPE BATTER: ENTREE I
SUGGESTED CREPE FOLD: TRADITIONAL

SWEET AND PUNGENT CHICKEN CREPES

1-1/2 cups (360 ml)
    spaghetti sauce
1/4 cup (120 ml) purple
    grape jam
2 tablespoons (30 ml) finely
    chopped onion
1 tablespoon (15 ml) lemon juice

2 teaspoons (10 ml)
    Worcestershire sauce
2 teaspoons (10 ml) prepared
    mustard
1/4 teaspoon (1.5 ml) salt
2 cups (480 ml) cooked
    chicken, minced

8 crepes

Combine all ingredients except chicken in frypan. Simmer, stirring occasionally, for 15 minutes. Add chicken and heat about 5 minutes. Spoon filling onto crepes. Fold and serve. Garnish with candied or fresh kumquats.

Makes 4 servings of 2 crepes each.

SUGGESTED CREPE BATTER: ENTREE II

SUGGESTED CREPE FOLD: TRADITIONAL

TURKEY AVOCADO CREPES

2 cups (480 ml) Medium White Sauce
1/2 teaspoon (2.5 ml) Worcestershire
1 cup (240 ml) grated Swiss cheese
2 tablespoons (30 ml) white wine
3 cups (720 ml) turkey, sliced
1/2 cup (120 ml) sliced ripe olives

1/4 cup (60 ml) diced
    canned pimiento
Salt and pepper
Large avocado, peeled
    and sliced

8 crepes

Prepare Medium White Sauce and combine with Worcestershire, 3/4 cup Swiss cheese and wine. Reserve 1/2 cup White Sauce and combine remainder with turkey, olives and pimiento. Season to taste with salt and pepper. Spoon onto crepes, fold, and place in greased baking dish. Arrange avocado over crepes. Spoon on remaining White Sauce and sprinkle with the rest of the cheese. Bake at 350° F. (177° C.) for 15 minutes. Broil to brown top. Garnish with watercress. Makes 4 servings of 2 crepes each.

SUGGESTED CREPE BATTER: ENTREE I

SUGGESTED CREPE FOLD: TRADITIONAL

1 tablespoon (15 ml) butter
  or margarine
1 cup (240 ml) beer
4 teaspoons (20 ml) flour
1 pound (455 g) sharp Cheddar
  cheese, grated
2 eggs, slightly beaten

2 teaspoons (10 ml)
  Worcestershire sauce
1/4 teaspoon (1.5 ml) salt
1/2 teaspoon (2.5 ml) paprika
1/2 teaspoon (2.5 ml) prepared mustard
Dash pepper
2 cups (480 ml) cooked turkey,
  diced

8 crepes

Melt butter in saucepan. Combine 1/4 cup (60 ml) beer with flour; stir in remaining beer. Add mixture to saucepan and heat until boiling, stirring constantly. Remove from heat and add grated cheese, stirring in a little at a time. Continue stirring until cheese is melted. Gradually stir in beaten eggs. Add Worcestershire, salt, paprika, mustard and salt, stirring over medium heat until thickened. Combine turkey with one cup of sauce. Spoon mixture onto crepes. Fold and place in baking dish. Spoon remaining sauce over crepes and bake at 350° F. (177° C.) for 10 to 20 minutes, or until sauce is bubbling and filling hot.

Makes 4 servings of 2 crepes each.
SUGGESTED CREPE BATTER: NUTTY CREPE
SUGGESTED CREPE FOLD: TRADITIONAL

Note: Recipes for sauces which are listed as ingredients in many of the entree crepes may be found in the Sauce chapter.

SEAFOOD

Cauliflower and Shrimp Crepes
Clamdiggers
Coquille St. Jacques Crepes
Crabmeat Bechamel Crepes
Crabmeat Salad Crepes
Creamed Salmon Crepes
Fisherman's Fillet Crepes
Jambalaya Crepes
Neptune Crepes
Quick Creamed Salmon Crepes
Saucy Scallop Crepes
Saucy Shrimp Crepes
Sherried Shrimp-Artichoke Crepes
Shrimp Oriental Crepes
Shrimp Stroganoff Crepes
South Seas Shrimp Crepes
Stuffed Seafood Crepes in Creole Sauce
Tuna Crepes Deluxe
Tuna Delight Crepes
Tuna Health Sandwiches

SEAFOOD CREPES

Turn fish haters into fish lovers. Whether you use fresh, frozen or canned seafood, you can make a spectacular variety of crepes that will get the less enthusiastic fish eater hooked on seafood.

Seafood crepes are also an answer for the calorie-conscious diner who must weigh his or her intake. Fish is low in calories and, if wrapped in a less rich crepe, one made from a batter with a minimum of butter or oil, with a dietetic sauce, produces delectable dining rather than just dull diet dishes.

Your favorite fish recipes should prove adaptable, too. Coquille St. Jacques, which we've included, is one example. Try your own recipes and see how wrapping them in a crepe adds dimension.

CAULIFLOWER AND SHRIMP CREPES

2 cups (480 ml) chopped
    cauliflower
2 cups (480 ml) milk
1 medium onion, chopped
2 sprigs of fresh dill
1/2 teaspoon (2.5 ml) salt
1/4 teaspoon (1.5 ml) pepper

1/4 cup (60 ml) butter
    or margarine
1/4 cup (60 ml) flour
2 cups (480 ml) cooked shrimp,
    shelled and chopped
3/4 cup (180 ml) heavy
    cream, whipped

8 crepes

Wash cauliflower, cook in boiling salted water. In saucepan, combine milk, onion and dill and bring to boil. Strain out dill. Add salt and pepper. Set aside. Melt butter and stir in flour, cooking until smooth — about 2 or 3 minutes. Gradually add milk, stirring constantly, over low heat. Add chopped shrimp and cook over low flame until heated. Fold in whipped cream. Spoon onto crepes. Fold. Spoon additional sauce over crepes and garnish with dill weed.

Makes 4 servings of 2 crepes each.
SUGGESTED CREPE BATTER: ENTREE II
SUGGESTED CREPE FOLD: POCKET

CLAMDIGGERS

2 10-ounce cans (560 g) chopped clams
2 medium-size potatoes, diced
2 medium-size onions, chopped
1/4 cup (60 ml) bread crumbs

1 cup (240 ml) milk
1 cup (240 ml) cream
Salt and pepper to taste

8 crepes

Drain clams and cook potatoes and onion in clam liquid until tender, about 10 to 15 minutes. Stir in bread crumbs. Add milk and cream slowly, allowing mixture to thicken after each addition. Add more bread crumbs if mixture is too thin and runny. Stir in clams, add salt and pepper. Spoon filling onto crepes. Fold. Place crepes in greased baking dish and spread remaining sauce over crepes. Bake at 375° F. (190° C.) for 20 minutes. Sprinkle with paprika and garnish with parsley before serving.

Makes 4 servings of 2 crepes each.
SUGGESTED CREPE BATTER: BEER
SUGGESTED CREPE FOLD: POCKET

COQUILLE ST. JACQUES CREPES

1 cup (240 ml) sliced mushrooms
1/4 cup (60 ml) sliced onion
1 tablespoon (15 ml) butter
    or margarine
Bechamel Sauce (without cloves)
1/2 pound (225 g) raw scallops
3/4 pound (340 g) shrimp,
    cooked and diced

1 cup (240 ml) flaked,
    cooked crab meat
2 tablespoons (30 ml) dry sherry
1 tablespoon (15 ml) lemon juice
Dash paprika
1 tablespoon (15 ml) grated
    Parmesan cheese

8 crepes

In frypan, saute mushrooms and onion in butter. Reserve 1/2 cup Bechamel Sauce, add sauteed vegetables to remainder. Cut large scallops in pieces; saute. Add scallops, shrimp, crab meat, sherry, lemon juice and paprika to sauce with mushrooms. Spoon onto crepes and fold. Place in greased baking dish. Pour remaining sauce over crepes, sprinkle with cheese. Bake at 350° F. (177° C.) for 15 minutes until hot. Broil to brown cheese. Garnish with parsley.

Makes 4 servings of two crepes each.
SUGGESTED CREPE BATTER: ENTREE I
SUGGESTED CREPE FOLD: TRADITIONAL

CRABMEAT BECHAMEL CREPES

3 tablespoons (45 ml) butter
3 tablespoons (45 ml) flour
1 cup (240 ml) chicken bouillon
1/2 cup (120 ml) light cream
1 egg yolk

1 tablespoon (15 ml) sherry
1-1/2 cups (360 ml) crabmeat,
    cooked and cubed
1/2 cup (120 ml) sliced
    mushrooms, sauteed
Paprika

8 crepes

In saucepan, melt butter over low heat. Add flour, stirring constantly until smooth and bubbly. Remove from heat. Add bouillon and light cream. Return to heat, stirring constantly. Add small amount of heated mixture to egg yolk. Stir. Pour into bouillon mixture, continuing to stir until thickened. Add sherry, crabmeat and mushrooms. Heat. Spoon onto crepe and fold. Top with additional mixture and sprinkle with paprika. Garnish with watercress.

Makes 4 servings of 2 crepes each.
SUGGESTED CREPE BATTER: ENTREE II
SUGGESTED CREPE FOLD: TRADITIONAL

CRABMEAT SALAD CREPES

13-ounces (370 g) cooked crabmeat
1/4 cup (60 ml) mayonnaise
1/3 cup (80 ml) celery
2 teaspoons (10 ml) white horseradish

2 tablespoons (30 ml) chopped
    green onion
1/4 teaspoon (1.5 ml) white pepper
2 teaspoons (10 ml) chopped parsley

8 crepes

Combine all ingredients except parsley in small mixing bowl. Cover and chill. Spoon mixture onto crepe. Fold. Garnish with dollop of mayonnaise and sprinkle with parsley.

Makes 4 servings of 2 crepes each.
SUGGESTED CREPE BATTER: ENTREE II
SUGGESTED CREPE FOLD: TRADITIONAL

CREAMED SALMON CREPES

1 small onion, chopped
2/3 cup (160 ml) thinly
   sliced celery
2 tablespoons (30 ml) butter
   or margarine
1 cup (240 ml) Medium
   White Sauce
1 tablespoon (15 ml) dry
   sherry, optional

1-1/2 teaspoon (7.5 ml)
   Dijon-style mustard
Dash salt
2-3 drops bottled hot
   pepper sauce
16-ounce can (455 g) salmon, drained
1-1/2 tablespoon (20 ml) milk
2 tablespoons, (30 ml) grated
   Parmesan cheese

8 crepes

In frypan, saute onion and celery in butter until crisp-tender. Add 2/3 cup white sauce, sherry, mustard, salt and hot pepper sauce, mix well. Remove all bones and skin from salmon and break into chunks. Carefully fold into sauce mixture. Spoon into crepes, fold and place in greased baking dish. Thin remaining white sauce with milk and pour over crepes. Sprinkle with cheese and bake at 375° F. (190° C.) for 10 minutes or until hot. Broil to brown cheese. Garnish with watercress or parsley.

Makes 4 servings of 2 crepes each.
SUGGESTED CREPE BATTER: ENTREE II
SUGGESTED CREPE FOLD: TRADITIONAL

FISHERMAN'S FILLET CREPES

1 pound (455 g) fish fillets
   (sole, perch or haddock)
Salt and pepper to taste
2 green onions, sliced
1/4 cup (60 ml) white wine or sherry
1 cup (240 ml) fresh mushrooms
   sliced, thin

3 tablespoons (45 ml) butter
2 tablespoons (30 ml) flour
2 egg yolks
1 cup (240 ml) light cream
1/2 teaspoon (2.5 ml) dill weed

8 crepes

Sprinkle fillets with salt and pepper. Bake with onions and wine in shallow greased baking dish at 400° F. (205° C.) for 15 to 20 minutes. Remove from oven. Drain juices and set aside. Cut fillets into small pieces and keep warm. In frypan, saute mushrooms in butter. Stir in flour and cook for about five minutes, or until bubbly. Add the fish juices, stirring constantly until thickened. In medium bowl, beat egg yolks with cream. Add dill. Stir a small amount of the hot mushroom mixture into eggs. Add egg mixture to frypan. Cook, stirring constantly, until thickened. Add fillets. Spoon about 3 or 4 tablespoons onto each crepe. Fold. Spoon remaining sauce over crepes. Garnish with thin lemon rounds dusted with paprika.

Makes 4 servings of 2 crepes each.
SUGGESTED CREPE BATTER: ENTREE II
SUGGESTED CREPE FOLD: TRADITIONAL

JAMBALAYA CREPES

3/4 cups (180 ml) regular long
   grain rice, uncooked
1 teaspoon (5 ml) salt
1 teaspoon (5 ml) Worcestershire
   sauce
1/8 teaspoon (1 ml) hot
   pepper sauce
1/8 teaspoon (1 ml) black pepper

1-1/2 cups (360 ml) chicken broth
1/2 cup (120 ml) green
   pepper, chopped
1/4 cup (60 ml) onion chopped
1 small garlic, minced
1/2 pound (255 g) cooked
   shrimp, shelled
3/4 cup (180 ml) ham

8 crepes

Preheat oven to 350° F. (177° C.). Grease casserole dish (8x6x2) and distribute uncooked rice on bottom of dish. Add all seasonings, onion and garlic, chicken broth and green pepper. Layer shrimp and ham on top. Bake in covered casserole for 1-1/2 hours. Rice should be light and fluffy. Spoon mixture onto crepes and fold. Garnish with parsley.

Makes 4 servings of 2 crepes each.
SUGGESTED CREPE BATTER: ENTREE II
SUGGESTED CREPE FOLD: TRADITIONAL

NEPTUNE CREPES

1-1/2 recipe Medium White Sauce
3 tablespoons (45 ml) finely
   chopped parsley (optional)
2 tablespoons (30 ml) dry sherry
1-1/2 teaspoons (7.5 ml) lemon juice
1/8 teaspoon (1 ml) paprika

2 cups (480 ml) cooked seafood,
   broken into bite-size pieces
   (shrimp, sole, halibut,
   flounder, lobster,
   scallops, etc.)
1/3 cup (80 ml) Parmesan cheese

8 crepes

Combine Medium White Sauce with parsley, sherry, lemon juice and paprika. Reserve 1/2 cup sauce. Fold seafood into remaining sauce. Spoon mixture onto crepes, and fold. Place in greased baking dish and spoon reserved sauce over crepes. Sprinkle with cheese and bake at 350° F. (177° C.) for 20 minutes, or until browned. Garnish with thinly sliced lemon sprinkled with paprika.

Makes 4 servings of 2 crepes each.
SUGGESTED CREPE BATTER: ENTREE II
SUGGESTED CREPE FOLD: TRADITIONAL

QUICK CREAMED SALMON CREPES

10-ounce package (285 g) frozen onions in cream sauce
2 cups (480 ml) salmon, flaked
4 tablespoons (60 ml) butter
1/2 pound (225 g) mushrooms, sliced thin
Salt and pepper to taste
1/2 cup (120 ml) Parmesan cheese

8 crepes

Prepare onions according to directions on package. Drain salmon and flake, add to cooked onions. Meanwhile, melt butter in frypan. Add mushrooms and saute until done, about 5 minutes. Add salmon and onion mixture. Salt and pepper to taste. Cook for additional 2 minutes. Spoon filling onto crepes. Fold. Place in greased baking dish and spoon remaining mixture over crepes. Sprinkle with cheese. Bake in preheated 350° F. (177° C.) oven for about 10 to 15 minutes. Garnish with pimiento strips.

Makes 4 servings of 2 crepes each.
SUGGESTED CREPE BATTER: ENTREE I
SUGGESTED CREPE FOLD: FRY

SAUCY SCALLOP CREPES

2 pounds (910 g) scallops
2 tablespoons (30 ml) butter or margarine
2/3 cup (160 ml) bottled chili sauce
1/3 cup (80 ml) catsup
2 tablespoons (30 ml) chopped parsley (optional)
2 tablespoons (30 ml) chopped parsley (optional)
1 tablespoon (15 ml) lemon juice
1 tablespoon (15 ml) Worcestershire
1-1/2 teaspoon (7.5 ml) prepared mustard
Dash pepper

8 crepes

In frypan, saute scallops in butter until brown and tender. Combine remaining ingredients and add to scallops. Heat to boiling. Spoon onto crepes, fold, and serve. Garnish with parsley.

Makes 4 servings of 2 crepes each.
SUGGESTED CREPE BATTER: ENTREE II
SUGGESTED CREPE FOLD: TRADITIONAL

SAUCY SHRIMP CREPES

2 medium-size zucchini, diced
1 shallot or scallion,
   finely chopped
2 tablespoons (30 ml) butter
   or margarine
3 tomatoes, peeled, seeded
   and chopped
3/4 teaspoon (7.5 ml) paprika

1/4 teaspoon (1.5 ml) salt
Dash pepper
1-1/2 pound (680 g) shrimp,
   cooked, peeled and deveined
Mornay Sauce
1/2 teaspoon (2.5 ml) Dijon-
   style mustard
2 tablespoons (30 ml) Parmesan cheese

8 crepes

In frypan, saute zucchini and shallot in butter. Add tomatoes and seasonings; saute 3-5 minutes more, or until zucchini is tender and most of liquid has evaporated. Dice shrimp and add to tomato mixture. Spoon mixture onto crepes and fold. Place in greased baking dish. Combine Mornay Sauce and mustard and pour over crepes. Sprinkle with cheese. Bake at 350° F. (177° C.) for 15 minutes, or until hot and lightly browned. Garnish with spears of raw zucchini sprinkled with paprika.

Makes 8 individual crepes.
SUGGESTED CREPE BATTER: ENTREE I
SUGGESTED CREPE FOLD: TRADITIONAL

SHERRIED SHRIMP-ARTICHOKE CREPES

10-ounce pkge. (285 g) frozen
   artichoke hearts
3/4 pound (340 g) sliced
   fresh mushrooms
2 tablespoons (30 ml) butter
   or margarine
1/4 cup (60 ml) dry sherry
2 teaspoons (10 ml) Worcestershire

2 cups (480 ml) Medium
   White Sauce
1-1/2 pounds (680 g.) frozen, cleaned
   shrimp, cooked and diced,
   or 2 cups (480 ml) diced,
   cooked fresh shrimp
1/3 cup (80 ml) grated
   Parmesan cheese

8 crepes

Cook artichoke hearts according to package directions, cut in half. In frypan, saute mushrooms in butter. Stir sherry and Worcestershire into Medium White Sauce. Combine artichokes, mushrooms, shrimp and about 1-1/4 cups sauce; stir gently. Spoon onto crepes, fold, and place in greased baking dish. Pour remaining sauce over crepes; sprinkle with Parmesan cheese. Bake at 350' F. (177° C.) for 15 minutes, or until hot and browned on top. Garnish with sliced fresh mushrooms sprinkled with paprika.

Makes 4 servings of 2 crepes each.
SUGGESTED CREPE BATTER: ENTREE I
SUGGESTED CREPE FOLD: TRADITIONAL

SHRIMP ORIENTAL

1 cup (240 ml) Oriental
  Duck Sauce
1/4 cup (60 ml) cola
1/4 cup (60 ml) mixed
  sweet pickles

2 tablespoons (30 ml) soy sauce
2 cups (480 ml) shrimp,
  cooked and shelled
1/2 cup (120 ml) pineapple chunks

8 crepes

Cook Duck Sauce thinned with cola in a saucepan over a slow fire until warm. Add sweet pickles and soy sauce, stirring constantly until bubbly. Stir in shrimp and pineapple chunks. Cook until warm. Spoon mixture into crepe. Pour additional sauce over crepes. Garnish with pineapple chunks and maraschino cherry on wooden spears.

Makes 4 servings of 2 crepes each.
SUGGESTED CREPE BATTER: ENTREE I
SUGGESTED CREPE FOLD: TRADITIONAL

SHRIMP STROGANOFF CREPES

1 medium onion, chopped
1 clove garlic, minced
1/2 pound (225 g) fresh
  mushrooms, sliced
3 tablespoons (45 ml) butter
  or margarine
2 tablespoons (30 ml) flour

3/4 teaspoon (3.5 ml) salt
1/4 teaspoon (1.5 ml) dill weed
1/2 cup (120 ml) beef broth
2 cups (480 ml) cooked
  diced shrimp
1/2 cup (120 ml) yogurt,
  room temperature

8 crepes

In frypan, saute onion, garlic and mushrooms in butter. Add flour, salt and dill weed. Remove from heat and gradually stir in beef broth until sauce is smooth. Cook until thickened, stirring constantly. Add shrimp and heat. Stir in yogurt and heat. Do not boil. Spoon onto crepes, fold and serve with sprig of fresh dill weed.

Makes 4 servings of 2 crepes each.
SUGGESTED CREPE BATTER: ENTREE I
SUGGESTED CREPE FOLD: TRADITIONAL

SOUTH SEAS SHRIMP CREPES

2 teaspoons (10 ml) cider vinegar
1 clove garlic, crushed
1-1/2 teaspoon (7.5 ml) ground
    coriander
3/4 teaspoon (3.5 ml) salt
1/4 teaspoon (1.5 ml) ground cumin
1/4 teaspoon (1.5 ml) ground
    tumeric
1/4 teaspoon (1.5 ml) mustard
Dash ground ginger
Dash cloves
Dash cayenne pepper
Dash nutmeg

2 pounds (910 g) fresh shrimp,
    shelled, deveined
    and cut in half
1/2 cup (120 ml) flaked coconut
1/2 cup (120 ml) milk
1 tablespoon (15 ml) confectioner's sugar
1 small onion, chopped
1 tablespoon (15 ml) butter
    or margarine
1 tablespoon (15 ml) flour
Juice of 1 lemon

8 crepes

Combine vinegar, garlic and spices. Add shrimp and toss gently. Cover and chill at least 2 hours. In the meantime combine coconut and milk; let stand 45 minutes. Drain, reserving milk and coconut. Mix coconut with confectioner's sugar and bake in 350° F. (177° C.) oven until brown, stirring occasionally. In frypan, saute onion in butter. Add shrimp mixture to onions and saute slowly until shrimp is done. Combine reserved milk with flour and stir into shrimp mixture. Cook to thicken. Add lemon juice. Spoon onto crepes, fold and sprinkle with toasted coconut. Serve immediately.

Makes 4 servings of 2 crepes each.
SUGGESTED CREPE BATTER: ENTREE I
SUGGESTED CREPE FOLD: TRADITIONAL

STUFFED SEAFOOD CREPES IN CREOLE SAUCE

Creole Sauce:

2 cups (480 ml) Marinara Sauce
1 small green pepper, chopped
1/4 cup (60 ml) sliced pimiento-
    stuffed olives

1/2 teaspoon (2.5 ml)
    Worcestershire

Filling:

1 cup (240 ml) cooked crab
1 cup (240 ml), diced,
    cooked shrimp

1/2 cup (120 ml) cooked
    flaked fillet of
    sole or flounder

8 to 10 crepes

Prepare Marinara Sauce, omitting oregano and basil. Add olives, green pepper and Worcestershire to the sauce. Simmer 30 minutes. Combine seafood, add 3/4 cup Creole Sauce, mix gently. Spoon seafood mixture into crepes, fold, and place in greased baking dish. Pour remaining sauce over top. Bake at 350° F. (177° C.) for 15-20 minutes or until hot. Garnish with pimiento sticks.

Makes 4 to 5 servings of 2 crepes each.
SUGGESTED CREPE BATTER: ENTREE I
SUGGESTED CREPE FOLD: TRADITIONAL

TUNA CREPES DELUXE

9-ounce pkg. (255 g) frozen
   mixed vegetables
7-ounce can (200 g) tuna, drained

1 cup (240 ml) Medium White Sauce
1/3 cup (80 ml) Parmesan cheese

8 crepes

Prepare vegetables according to package directions. Drain. Add tuna and vegetables to White Sauce and heat. Spoon onto crepes; fold. Sprinkle cheese over crepes. Serve garnished with small onions.

Makes 4 servings of 2 crepes each.
SUGGESTED CREPE BATTER: ONION
SUGGESTED CREPE FOLD: TRADITIONAL

TUNA DELIGHT CREPES

7-1/2 ounce can (210) tuna,
   drained
1/2 cup (120 ml) cracker crumbs
1 egg beaten
1 tablespoon (15 ml) mayonnaise
1 tablespoon (15 ml) finely
   chopped onion
1 tablespoon (15 ml) finely
   chopped celery

1 tablespoon (15 ml) finely chopped
   green pepper
1 tablespoon (15 ml) finely
   chopped carrot
1/4 teaspoon (1.5 ml) salt
Dash pepper
Paprika
10-1/2 ounce can (300 ml) cream of
   celery soup, undiluted

8 crepes

Combine all ingredients except soup. Mix well. Blend in 1/4 can soup. Spoon mixture onto crepes, fold, and place in greased baking dish. Bake at 350° F. (177° C.) for 15 minutes, or until hot. Heat remaining soup, undiluted, and serve as sauce. Dust with paprika and garnish with thin slices of olives.

Makes 4 servings of 2 crepes each.
SUGGESTED CREPE BATTER: ENTREE II
SUGGESTED CREPE FOLD: TRADITIONAL

7-ounce can (200 ml) tuna, drained
1/4 cup (60 g) finely minced
   green pepper
2 tablespoons (30 ml) chopped
   scallion

1/2 teaspoon (2.5 ml) horseradish
Salt and pepper to taste
2 tablespoons (30 ml) mayonnaise
2/3 cup (160 ml) alfalfa sprouts

4 crepes

Combine tuna, green pepper, scallion and horseradish, season to taste with salt and pepper. Stir in mayonnaise to moisten. Spread crepes with tuna mixture, sprinkle with alfalfa sprouts and roll up. Serve immediately, garnished with cherry tomatoes.

Makes 4 individual servings.

SUGGESTED CREPE BATTER: ENTREE II
SUGGESTED CREPE FOLD: SPIRAL ROLL

Note: Recipes for sauces which are listed as ingredients in many of the entree crepes may be found in the Sauce chapter.

INTERNATIONAL FAVORITES

FROM CHINA	Moo Shu Pork
	Pork Shrimp Subgum
FROM ENGLAND	Yorkshire Crepes
FROM FINLAND	Finnish Herring Salad in Crepes
FROM FRANCE	Lobster Newburg Parisian
FROM GERMANY	Bavarian Specials
FROM GREECE	Gyros
	Moussaka
FROM HUNGARY	Hungarian Veal Crepes
FROM INDIA	Indian Curried Turkey
FROM ITALY	Cannelloni
	Italiano Crepes
	Ravioli-Cheese
	Ravioli-Meat
FROM MEXICO	Enchiladas
	Frijoles
	Mock Bean Tamale
FROM THE	
MIDDLE EAST	Armenian Meatball Crepes
FROM NORWAY	Mideastern Lamb Stew in Crepes
FROM RUSSIA	Norwegian Meat Salad
FROM SWEDEN	Crepes Stroganoff
	Swedish Meatballs

Take your family and your friends on a food tour around the world . . . with crepes. Serve a Mexican or Scandinavian dinner, an exotic Polynesian repast or an Italian feast. While crepes are international from appetizers to desserts, a crepe dish for every course might be a bit much. So try one of these favorite entrees to set the theme. Or if you're having a party, be international and serve a selection of foods from around the world in crepes.

CHINA

MOO SHU PORK

1/2 cup (120 ml) lily buds, optional (available in gourmet shops)
1/4 cup (60 ml) dried black mushrooms
4 tablespoons (60 ml) peanut oil
1 pound (455 g) lean pork, shredded
4 eggs, lightly beaten
4 tablespoons (60 ml) bamboo shoots, shredded

2 scallions (shred white and chop green in 1/2 inch pieces)
4 snow pea pods, cut fine
4 water chestnuts, sliced thin
2 tablespoons (30 ml) soy sauce
2 tablespoons (30 ml) sugar
2 tablespoons (30 ml) dry sherry
1/2 teaspoon (2.5 ml) salt

8 crepes

Soak lily buds and mushrooms in separate bowls in hot water for 15 minutes. In frypan, heat peanut oil over high flame and stir-fry shredded pork and bamboo shoots until pork turns "white." Remove with slotted spoon and set aside. In same oil, scramble eggs, breaking into very small pieces. Remove eggs while still moist. Drain lily buds and mushrooms. Slice mushrooms into very thin pieces and add to lily buds. Add in scallions, pea pods and water chestnuts. Stir-fry mixture in frypan, adding more oil if necessary. Stir in soy sauce, sugar, dry sherry and salt. Cover and cook for 1 to 2 minutes over medium heat. Add pork and scrambled eggs. Heat thoroughly. Serve crepes and pork mixture separately, allowing guests to fill and fold their own crepes.

Makes 4 servings of 2 crepes each.
SUGGESTED CREPE BATTER: ENTREE I
SUGGESTED CREPE FOLD: FLAT

PORK SHRIMP SUBGUM

1 tablespoon (15 ml) cornstarch
1/2 cup (120 ml) cold
    chicken stock
1/2 pound (225 g) pork,
    chopped fine
2 tablespoons (30 ml) peanut oil
1/2 pound (225 g) shrimp,
    cooked and chopped

1 tablespoon (15 ml) soy sauce
1 tablespoon (15 ml) sherry
1 teaspoon (5 ml) salt
1 green onion, including
    top, chopped
1 medium can chopped
    Chinese vegetables

8 crepes

Combine cornstarch with cold chicken stock in small bowl, and set aside. In frypan, fry pork in peanut oil over medium heat for five minutes. Add shrimp, soy sauce, sherry, salt, green onion and Chinese vegetables. Heat thoroughly. Add cornstarch mixture to frypan and cook until mixture thickens. Spoon onto crepe, fold. Garnish with chopped salted peanuts, Chinese mustard and plum sauce.

Makes 4 servings of 2 crepes each.
SUGGESTED CREPE BATTER: ENTREE I
SUGGESTED CREPE FOLD: TRADITIONAL

ENGLAND

YORKSHIRE CREPES

1 pound (455 g) roast beef,
    thinly sliced
Salt and pepper

1 cup (240 ml) sour cream
1-1/2 tablespoons (20 ml)
    white horseradish

8 crepes

Arrange one or two slices of roast beef on each crepe. Add dash of salt and pepper to beef. Fold crepe. Place crepes in shallow baking pan, cover with foil, and heat in 350° F. (177° C.) oven for about 10 minutes, or until warm. Combine sour cream and horseradish. Spoon mixture over hot crepes. Garnish with cherry tomatoes or parsley.

Makes 4 servings of 2 crepes each.
SUGGESTED CREPE BATTER: ENTREE II
SUGGESTED CREPE FOLD: HALF

FINLAND

FINNISH HERRING SALAD IN CREPES

2 medium size herring fillets
1-1/2 cups (360 ml) cooked
   beets, sliced
1 cup (240 ml) cooked
   carrots, diced
1 cup (240 ml) roast beef, diced
2 medium-size dill pickles, diced

2 unpeeled tart
   apples, diced
2 tablespoons (30 ml) raisins
2 hard-cooked
   eggs, chopped
1 recipe dressing

DRESSING

1 cup (240 ml) heavy cream
1 tablespoon (15 ml) sugar
2 tablespoons (30 ml) lemon juice

1 teaspoon (5 ml) dried mustard
Salt and pepper to taste

8 crepes

Wash herring. Drain. Cut into small pieces. Combine with beets, carrots, beef, pickles, apples, raisins and eggs. Refrigerate. Prepare dressing. Mix with salad. Chill. To serve, spoon mixture onto crepe, fold. Garnish with slices of hard-boiled egg and pickled beets.

Makes 4 servings of 2 crepes each.
SUGGESTED CREPE BATTER: ENTREE I
SUGGESTED CREPE FOLD: SPIRAL

FRANCE

LOBSTER NEWBURG PARISIAN

12 ounces (340 g) chopped lobster
2 tablespoons (30 ml) margarine
   or butter
2 tablespoons (30 ml) flour
1/2 teaspoon (2.5 ml) salt
1/4 teaspoon (1.5 ml) white pepper

1 cup (240 ml) light cream
1 egg yolk
2 tablespoons (30 ml) Parmesan cheese
1 tablespoon (15 ml) dry sherry
Dash ground nutmeg

8 crepes

In frypan, saute lobster until opaque—about 3 minutes. Remove lobster. Blend flour, salt and pepper into margarine remaining in frypan. Stir in cream gradually; cook until mixture boils. Stir some of hot mixture quickly into egg yolk. Return egg mixture to sauce; add 2 tablespoons cheese to sauce remaining in frypan. Cook 1 minute longer, stirring. Stir in lobster, sherry and nutmeg. Fill crepe with 2 tablespoons of mixture, and fold. Top with any excess mixture and sprinkle with additional Parmesan cheese. Garnish with parsley.

Makes 4 servings of 2 crepes each.
SUGGESTED CREPE BATTER: ENTREE II
SUGGESTED CREPE FOLD: TRADITIONAL

GERMANY

8 ounces (225 g) sauerkraut
1/2 cup (120 ml) white
 corn syrup
2 tablespoons (30 ml)
 tomato paste
2 tablespoons (30 ml) caraway seeds

4 knockwurst or bratwurst
1/2 cup (120 ml) brown
 mustard
1/4 cup (60 ml) white
 horseradish

8 crepes

Drain and wash sauerkraut. Cook about 1 hour over slow heat, until very soft. Add corn syrup, tomato paste, and caraway seeds. Cut knockwurst in half along length. Add to sauerkraut. Cook until heated, about 5 minutes. Remove from heat. Drain liquid from sauerkraut. Spoon sauerkraut and 1/2 knockwurst onto each crepe. Fold. Mix brown mustard and horseradish together. Spoon on top as garnish.

Makes 4 servings of 2 crepes each.
SUGGESTED CREPE BATTER: POTATO
SUGGESTED CREPE FOLD: TRADITIONAL

GREECE

1 pound (455 g) ground lamb
1 pound (455 g) ground beef
2 tablespoons (30 ml) olive oil
1 medium onion
1/2 teaspoon (2.5 ml) crushed
 oregano

1 clove garlic, crushed
1/2 teaspoon (2.5 ml) black pepper
1 tomato, cut in wedges
1 lemon, cut in wedges

8 crepes

In frypan, brown ground lamb and beef in olive oil. Add onion and seasonings. Cook until onions are tender. Drain grease. Spoon mixture onto crepe, and fold. Garnish with tomato wedge and lemon wedge. Lemon juice on the crepe will also add to its flavor.

Makes 4 servings of 2 crepes each.
SUGGESTED CREPE BATTER: ENTREE I
SUGGESTED CREPE FOLD: TRADITIONAL

2 cups (480 ml) unpeeled
   eggplant, diced
Salt to taste
2 tablespoons (30 ml) oil
1 pound (455 g) ground lamb
1 tablespoon (15 ml) butter
  or margarine
Dash cinnamon

2 large tomatoes, peeled, seeded
   and chopped
3 tablespoons (45 ml) dry bread crumbs
1-1/2 cups (360 ml) Bechamel Sauce
2 egg yolks
1/3 cup (80 ml) Parmesan
   cheese, grated

8 to 10 crepes

Sprinkle eggplant with salt and let stand 15 minutes to remove moisture. Rinse, drain on paper towels. Brown eggplant in hot oil, remove and drain. Brown meat in butter, add 1/2 teaspoon salt, the cinnamon and tomatoes. Simmer until tomatoes are soft and liquid has evaporated. Stir in bread crumbs. Combine Bechamel Sauce with egg yolks. Add half the sauce and half the grated cheese to the eggplant. Spoon both the meat and the eggplant mixtures onto crepes. Fold, and place in greased baking dish. Pour remaining sauce over crepes and sprinkle with remaining cheese. Bake at 350° F. (177° C.) for 20 to 25 minutes, or until bubbly and crisp on top.

Makes 4 or 5 servings of 2 crepes each.
SUGGESTED CREPE BATTER: ENTREE I
SUGGESTED CREPE FOLD: TRADITIONAL

HUNGARY

HUNGARIAN VEAL CREPES

3 tablespoons (45 ml) butter
  or margarine
1 cup (240 ml) onions, minced
1/2 pound (225 g) fresh
   mushrooms, thinly sliced
1 pound (455 g) veal fillets

1/2 teaspoon (2.5 ml) salt
2 tablespoons (30 ml) red paprika
1 cup (240 ml) beef stock
1/2 cup (120 ml) sour cream
1/2 teaspoon (2.5 ml) cornstarch

8 crepes

Melt butter or margarine in frypan. Add onions and mushrooms and saute until tender. Add veal, salt and paprika. Saute about 2 minutes over high heat. Add stock and bring to a boil. Reduce heat and simmer, covered, for about 30 minutes, or until meat is tender. Remove meat from sauce. Cut into small pieces and set aside. Combine sour cream and cornstarch and add to hot gravy. Cook over low heat, stirring, until sauce thickens. Remove from heat and add meat. Spoon mixture onto each crepe. Fold. Place crepes in greased baking dish and bake in preheated 375° F. (190° C.) oven for 10 to 15 minutes. Garnish with raw mushrooms and dust with paprika.

Makes 4 servings of 2 crepes each.
SUGGESTED CREPE BATTER: ENTREE I
SUGGESTED CREPE FOLD: TRADITIONAL

INDIA

INDIAN CURRIED TURKEY

2 tablespoons (30 ml) minced onion
1 tablespoon (15 ml) finely diced
   green pepper
1 tablespoon (15 ml) butter
   or margarine
3 tablespoons (45 ml) flour
1-1/4 teaspoons (6.5 ml)
   curry powder

1 cup (240 ml) turkey stock
   or chicken broth
2 cups (480 ml) diced,
   cooked turkey
3 tablespoons (45 ml) chopped peanuts
2 tablespoons (30 ml) chopped pimiento
Salt and pepper
1 small red apple, diced

8 crepes

In frypan, saute onion and green pepper in butter. Stir in flour and curry powder, cook 1 minute. Remove from heat and gradually add turkey stock, stirring constantly. Heat to boiling. Add turkey, peanuts and pimiento. Season to taste with salt and pepper. Add apple and cook 1 to 2 minutes, or until apple is crisp-tender. Spoon onto crepes. Fold. Serve immediately, garnished with chutney.

Makes 4 servings of two crepes each.
SUGGESTED CREPE BATTER: ENTREE I
SUGGESTED CREPE FOLD: TRADITIONAL

ITALY

Italiano and ravioli or cannelloni crepes are great when you're in the mood for Italian food. Serve any one as an entree, or serve one of each, accompanied by a tossed green salad, for a different kind of Italian dinner.

CANNELLONI

1 medium onion, chopped
1 clove garlic, minced
1/2 pound (225 g) boneless
   chicken, cut into
   1-inch pieces
1/4 pound (115 g) boneless lean
   veal, cut into
   1-inch pieces
2 tablespoons (30 ml) butter
   or margarine

2/3 cup (160 ml) ricotta cheese
1/3 cup (80 ml) grated
   Parmesan cheese
1 egg, beaten
1/2 teaspoon (2.5 ml) salt
Dash nutmeg
8-ounce can (225 g)
   tomato sauce
1/2 teaspoon (2.5 ml) basil
1/4 pound (115 g) mozzarella
   cheese, sliced

8 crepes

Brown onion, garlic, chicken and veal in butter in oven proof skillet. Bake at 350° F. (177° C.) for 15-20 minutes, or until meats are done. Cool. Force through a food chopper with ricotta, or finely chop meat and stir in ricotta. Add Parmesan cheese, egg, salt and nutmeg and mix well. Combine tomato sauce and basil; pour into greased baking dish. Spoon meat mixture onto crepes, fold and place in baking dish. Top with mozzarella cheese and bake at 350° F. (177° C.) for 15-20 minutes, or until hot and cheese is melted and browned. Garnish with parsley.

Makes 4 serving of 2 crepes each.
SUGGESTED CREPE BATTER: ENTREE I
SUGGESTED CREPE FOLD: TRADITIONAL

ITALIANO CREPES

1 pound (455 g) ground beef
1 medium onion, chopped
1/2 cup (120 ml) diced
   green pepper
2 tablespoons (30 ml) margarine
1 tablespoon (15 ml) Parmesan
   cheese, grated

Dash pepper
1/2 teaspoon (2.5 ml) garlic salt
1/4 teaspoon (1.5 ml) oregano
Pinch of fennel seed
1 cup (240 ml) cooked rice
2 8-ounce (455 g) cans tomato sauce
8 slices mozzarella cheese

8 crepes

In frypan, brown ground beef, onion and green pepper. Drain grease. Add seasonings, rice and tomato sauce to ground beef mixture. Stir to blend seasonings. Simmer, heating thoroughly. Place a slice of mozzarella cheese on crepe and spoon mixture over cheese. Fold crepe and spoon on additional tomato sauce seasoned with salt, pepper and oregano. Garnish with parsley.

RAVIOLI CREPES — CHEESE

3/4 pound (340 g) ricotta cheese
2 eggs, beaten
1/2 cup (120 ml) Parmesan
   cheese, grated

1/2 pound (225 g) mozzarella
   cheese, shredded
1/2 teaspoon (2.5 ml) salt
1/2 teaspoon (2.5 ml) parsley flakes

RAVIOLI CREPES — BEEF

1 pound (455 g) ground beef
1 medium onion, chopped
1 teaspoon (5 ml) salt

Marinara Sauce
1/2 cup (120 ml) mozzarella,
   shredded

6 to 8 crepes

Mix ricotta, eggs, Parmesan and mozzarella cheeses, salt and parsley. Brown ground beef in frypan. Add onion and salt and cook until tender. Drain grease. Spoon meat filling onto 3 or 4 crepes and cheese filling onto the remaining crepes. Fold. Coat bottom of individual casserole baking dishes with Marinara Sauce. Place crepes in dish. Top with Marinara Sauce and shredded mozzarella.

Makes 3 to 4 servings of 2 crepes each.
SUGGESTED CREPE BATTER: ENTREE I
SUGGESTED CREPE FOLD: POCKET

MEXICO

Treat friends or family to a Mexican dinner. One each of the following three crepes make up an exciting entree for a hearty yet gala meal.

ENCHILADAS

10-ounce can (285 g)
   enchilada sauce
4 cups (960 ml) grated Cheddar
   cheese
1/4 cup (60 ml) chopped onions

2 tablespoons (30 ml) chopped
   green chilies
Shredded lettuce
Sliced ripe olives

6 crepes

Pour 1/2 can of enchilada sauce in bottom of 9x9x2-inch pan. Dip cornmeal crepe in enchilada sauce. Mix cheese, onion and green chilies together. Place 1/4 cup cheese mixture on crepe. Roll crepe. Repeat procedure for next 5 crepes. Place rolled crepes in single layer in bottom of pan. Pour remaining half of enchilada sauce over crepes and top with remaining cheese. Bake in oven at 350° F. (177° C.) until cheese melts, about 30 minutes. Serve topped with shredded lettuce and sliced olives.

Makes 6 individual servings.
SUGGESTED CREPE BATTER: CORNMEAL
SUGGESTED CREPE FOLD: SPIRAL

FRIJOLES

15-ounce can (425 g) refried beans
1 teaspoon (5 ml) minced onion
1/2 cup (120 ml) grated
   Cheddar cheese

1 teaspoon (5 ml) chopped
   green chilies

6 crepes

Place beans, onions and chilies in frypan. Heat thoroughly. Spoon 2 tablespoons bean mixture onto crepe. Sprinkle with Cheddar cheese. Fold crepe and place in baking dish, repeat procedure with remaining crepes. Place crepes in a single layer and sprinkle with remaining cheese. Bake at 350° F. (177° C.) until cheese melts—about 15 minutes.

Makes 6 individual servings.
SUGGESTED CREPE BATTER: CORNMEAL
SUGGESTED CREPE FOLD: SPIRAL

15-ounce can (425 g) refried beans
1/4 cup (60 ml) brown
    sugar, packed
1/4 cup (60 ml) raisins
2 tablespoons (30 ml) water

6 crepes

Place all ingredients in frypan and heat thoroughly. Spoon 2 tablespoons bean mixture onto crepe. Fold. Clean frypan, then pour in one inch of oil. Heat oil to 375° F. (190° C.) and fry crepes until golden brown — about 1 minute each side.

Makes 6 individual servings.
SUGGESTED CREPE BATTER: CORNMEAL
SUGGESTED CREPE FOLD: FRY

MIDDLE EAST

ARMENIAN MEATBALL CREPES

1 egg, beaten
1 pound (455 g) ground lamb
1 clove garlic, crushed
1 small onion, minced
3/4 cup (180 ml) Cheddar cheese
1 cup (240 ml) soft bread crumbs
2 teaspoons (10 ml) parsley,
    chopped
1/8 teaspoon (1 ml) cinnamon
1/2 teaspoon (2.5 ml) salt
Dash pepper
2 tablespoons (30 ml) oil
8-ounce can (225 g)
    tomato sauce
Parmesan cheese

8 crepes

Combine egg, lamb, garlic, onion, Cheddar cheese, bread crumbs, parsley and seasonings thoroughly. Shape into balls about 1 inch in diameter. Brown in oil, a few at a time. Drain grease. Add tomato sauce and simmer 30 minutes. Spoon 2-3 meatballs onto each crepe, and fold. Place crepes in greased baking dish. Spoon a small amount of sauce over top, sprinkle with Parmesan cheese and broil to brown. Serve with remaining sauce. Garnish with parsley.

Makes 4 servings of 2 crepes each.
SUGGESTED CREPE BATTER: ENTREE I
SUGGESTED CREPE FOLD: TRADITIONAL

1-1/2 pounds (680 g) lean lamb
  stew meat, cut
  into 3/4-inch cubes
3 tablespoons (45 ml) oil
1 medium onion, chopped
2 cloves garlic, minced
3/4 cup (180 ml) water
1 chicken bouillon cube
1/2 teaspoon (2.5 ml) salt

1/8 teaspoon (1 ml) cayenne
Dash pepper
8-ounce can (225 g) small white
  onions, drained
4 teaspoons (20 ml) cornstarch
1/4 cup 60 ml) milk
1 egg, beaten
1-1/4 cups (300 ml) plain yogurt

8 crepes

Brown stew meat in hot oil in electric frypan. Add onion and garlic and brown slightly. Add water, bouillon cube and seasonings. Cover and simmer until tender, about 1 hour. Add onions and simmer 10 minutes longer. Combine cornstarch and milk and stir into meat. Cook until thickened. Lower heat, combine egg and yogurt and gradually stir into meat. Stir over very low heat until warm. Spoon onto crepes, fold, and serve immediately. Garnish with parsley.

Makes 4 servings of 2 crepes each.
SUGGESTED CREPE BATTER: ENTREE I
SUGGESTED CREPE FOLD: TRADITIONAL

NORWAY

1 cup (240 ml) roast beef,
  cut in julienne strips
1 cup (240 ml) boiled ham,
  cut in julienne strips
1 tablespoon (15 ml) minced onion
6 tablespoons (90 ml) salad oil

2 tablespoons (30 ml) lemon
Salt and pepper
1 teaspoon (5 ml) dill weed
1/4 cup (60 ml) dairy sour cream
2 hard-boiled eggs, sliced
2 pickled beets, sliced

8 crepes

Mix cut meats with onion. Mix oil, lemon, salt and pepper and dill. Stir sour cream into dressing. Toss with meats. Spoon onto crepes, top with sliced egg and beets. Fold. Garnish with dollop of sour cream and fresh sprig of dill.

Makes 4 servings of 2 crepes each.
SUGGESTED CREPE BATTER: ONION
SUGGESTED CREPE FOLD: TRADITIONAL

RUSSIA

CREPES STROGANOFF

1 pound (455 g) round steak,
   3/4-inch-thick slice
2 tablespoons (30 ml) flour
3/4 teaspoon (3.5 ml) salt
Dash pepper
2 tablespoons (30 ml) onion,
   finely chopped

1/2 pound (225 g) mushrooms,
   thinly sliced
1/2 teaspoon (2.5 ml) basil
1/4 cup (60 ml) white wine
1/2 cup (120 ml) beef bouillon
1/2 cup (120 ml) sour cream
2 tablespoons (15 ml) butter
   or margarine

8 crepes
Cut meat into slices about 1/4-inch thick. Combine flour, salt and pepper. Toss with meat. Brown meat and onion in butter. Push meat to one side of frypan and saute mushrooms briefly on other side. Add basil, wine and bouillon. Cover and simmer until tender, about 30 minutes. Add more bouillon as necessary. Remove from heat and stir in sour cream. Spoon onto crepes, fold and serve. Garnish with cherry tomatoes or chutney.

Makes 4 servings of 2 crepes each.
SUGGESTED CREPE BATTER: ENTREE I
SUGGESTED CREPE FOLD: TRADITIONAL

SWEDEN

A great smorgasboard dish. Serve with thinly sliced cucumbers in sour cream and dill, and an assortment of cold salads and cheeses.

SWEDISH MEATBALLS

4 tablespoons (60 ml) finely
   chopped onions
1 cup (240 ml) mashed potatoes
3 tablespoons (45 ml) dry bread
   crumbs
1 pound (455 g) ground beef

1/3 cup (80 ml) light cream
1/2 teaspoon (2.5 ml) salt
1 egg
1 teaspoon (5 ml) parsley
2 tablespoons (30 ml) butter
2 tablespoons (30 ml) oil

GRAVY

1 tablespoon (15 ml) flour

3/4 cups (180 ml) light cream

14 to 16 crepes
Combine onions, mashed potatoes, bread crumbs, meat, cream, salt, egg and parsley in medium bowl and shape into 1-inch meatballs. Chill one hour. Fry in butter and oil. To prepare gravy, combine flour with cream in saucepan, stirring to eliminate lumps. Cook over medium heat until thickened. Place 3 to 4 meatballs in each crepe. Fold. Top with gravy. Garnish with sprigs of fresh dill weed.

Makes up to 16 crepes.
SUGGESTED CREPE BATTER: ENTREE I
SUGGESTED CREPE FOLD: TRADITIONAL

VEGETABLE/CHEESE CREPES

Asparagus 'n' Cheese Crepes
Asparagus Souffle Crepes
Beefy Potato Crepes
Blue Cheese and Apple Crepes
Broccoli Crepes with Hot Meat Sauce
Broccoli with Cheese Sauce
Brussels Sprouts in Cheddar Sauce
Cabbage Strudel Crepes
Carrots in Cheese Sauce
Cheddar Plus Sandwiches
Cheese Blintzes Devine
Cheese Crepes Provencal
Creamy Zucchini Crepes
Crepes a la Waldorf
Divine Cheese Crepes
Easy Spinach Souffle Crepes
"Garden Greens" Crepes
Greek Spinach and Cheese Crepes

Green Beans Bechamel
Late Supper Crepes
Mandarin Vegetable Crepes
Mushroom Crepes
Nutty Squash Crepes
Pepperoni-Chick Pea Crepes
Potato Blintzes, Jewish Style
Ratatouille Crepes
Spicy Cheddar Crepes
Spinach Cheese Crepes
Spinach Crepes
Spinach Specials
Sweet-and-Sour Cabbage Crepes
Tomato-Okra Combo
Vegetable Creole Crepes
Vegetable Salad Vinaigrette
Zucchini Crepes

WRAPPING THINGS UP ... VEGETABLES WITH A DIFFERENCE

"I'm a meat and potatoes man," a friend recently announced as he helped himself to a fourth vegetable crepe. "Never did like vegetables," he continued, as the crepe quickly disappeared from his plate and he debated whether to reach for a fifth.

That's how vegetable haters react to vegetables wrapped in a crepe — because from everyday peas to elegant asparagus, vegetables take on a new taste dimension when wrapped in a crepe.

Time after time I've seen people eat vegetables only because they're nutritious. But most people enjoy as well as benefit from vegetables when they are prepared as part of a crepe dish.

When preparing vegetables in crepes, throw caution to the wind. Try new combinations and different sauces. Use fresh, frozen or canned vegetables. Give leftovers new life with an added vegetable or a sauce.

A vegetarian dinner is also a good way to go easy on your budget. Crepes are so delicious and filling no one will miss the meat. We've also included cheese in this section. Try some combinations of the cheese crepes and the vegetable crepes to make a meatless meal. It's a good "marriage."

Traditionally, crepes are not "stuffed" but are filled sparingly. However, the amount of filling you use in a single crepe depends on your taste. If you do have excess filling, use as a sauce or garnish.

ASPARAGUS 'N' CHEESE CREPES

1-1/2 cups (360 ml) asparagus,
  cut into 1-inch pieces
1/4 cup (60 ml)
  finely chopped onion

2 tablespoons (30 ml) butter
  or margarine
Salt and pepper to taste
1/4 teaspoon (1.5 ml) marjoram
1/4 pound (115 g) grated Swiss cheese
Mock Hollandaise Sauce

8 crepes

Cook asparagus until barely tender; drain. In frypan, stir-fry asparagus and onion in butter 2-3 minutes; season with salt and pepper. Add marjoram. Spoon asparagus and about 1-1/2 tablespoons grated cheese onto each crepe, fold and place in greased baking dish. Sprinkle remaining cheese over crepes. Bake at 375° F. (190° C.) for 10 minutes, or until cheese is melted and brown. Top with Mock Hollandaise Sauce.

Makes 4 individual servings.
SUGGESTED CREPE BATTER: NUTTY CREPE
SUGGESTED CREPE FOLD: TRADITIONAL

ASPARAGUS SOUFFLE CREPES

12-ounce package (340 g)
frozen asparagus souffle

Cheese Sauce or Mornay Sauce

4 crepes

Thaw frozen asparagus until soft enough to cut into 4 long strips. Transfer frozen strips to crepes, fold, and place in greased baking dish. Cover with foil, puncturing foil in several places with a fork. Bake in 375° F. (190° C.) oven for 35 minutes. Remove foil and bake 15-20 minutes longer, or until knife inserted in center of one crepe comes out clean. Serve with Cheese or Mornay Sauce. Garnish with parsley.

Makes four individual Servings.
SUGGESTED CREPE BATTER: ENTREE II
SUGGESTED CREPE FOLD: TRADITIONAL

BEEFY POTATO CREPES

2 medium onions, sliced
2 tablespoons (30 ml) butter
  or margarine
3 medium potatoes, diced

1/2 cup (120 ml) beef bouillon
Salt and pepper
Dash paprika

6 crepes

Saute onions in butter until tender. Add potatoes and bouillon. Sprinkle with salt, pepper and paprika. Cover and simmer, stirring occasionally, until potatoes are tender. Spoon onto crepes, fold, and serve immediately, garnished with parsley.

Makes 6 individual servings.
SUGGESTED CREPE BATTER: ENTREE I
SUGGESTED CREPE FOLD: TRADITIONAL

BLUE CHEESE AND APPLE CREPES

8 ounces (235 g) blue cheese
2 tablespoons (30 ml) milk

4 apples, cored and
  thinly sliced

8 crepes

Soften cheese with milk. Spread on crepes. Top with layer of apples, sliced paper thin. Fold. Place in greased baking dish and bake at 375° F. (190° C.) about 10 minutes. Garnish with more apple slices.

Makes 8 individual servings.
SUGGESTED CREPE BATTER: NUTTY CREPES
SUGGESTED CREPE FOLD: POCKET

BROCCOLI CREPES WITH HOT MEAT SAUCE

1 bunch broccoli
3 tablespoons (45 ml) chopped onion
2 tablespoons (30 ml) butter
   or margarine
1 pound (455 g) ground beef
8-ounce can (225 g) tomato sauce
1/2 teaspoon (2.5 ml) salt

1 clove garlic, crushed
1/4 teaspoon (1.5 ml) oregano
1/4 teaspoon (1.5 ml) basil
1 teaspoon (5 ml) chili powder
1/2 teaspoon (2.5 ml) dried
   crushed red pepper

6 crepes

Separate broccoli into flowerettes and cook in salted water until barely tender. Drain. In frypan, saute broccoli and onion in butter for 2-3 minutes. Set aside. Brown meat, drain grease. Add tomato sauce and seasonings. Simmer, covered, 30 minutes. Mixture will be thick. Spoon broccoli onto crepes, fold, and place in greased baking dish. Spoon meat sauce over ends of crepes; sprinkle meat with cheese. Bake at 350° F. (177° C.) for 10-15 minutes, or until cheese melts.

Makes 6 individual servings.

SUGGESTED CREPE BATTER: CORNMEAL

SUGGESTED CREPE FOLD: TRADITIONAL

BROCCOLI WITH CHEESE SAUCE

10-ounce package (285 g)
   frozen broccoli spears

Parmesan cheese
Cheese Sauce

8 crepes

Prepare broccoli as per package instructions. Drain, cut any large broccoli spears lengthwise into sections. Place 1 spear (or part of larger spear) on each crepe. Sprinkle with Parmesan cheese. Fold crepe. Top with Cheese Sauce.

Makes 8 individual servings.

SUGGESTED CREPE BATTER: ENTREE II

SUGGESTED CREPE FOLD: TRADITIONAL

BRUSSELS SPROUTS IN CHEDDAR SAUCE

10-ounce package (285 g) frozen
  Brussels sprouts
1/2 cup (120 ml) thinly
  sliced celery

1 cup (240 ml) Cheese Sauce,
  prepared with Cheddar cheese
1/3 cup (80 ml) grated
  Cheddar cheese

8 crepes

Combine Brussels sprouts and celery in saucepan. Cook according to package directions for sprouts. Drain. Slice sprouts in quarters. Add about half the cheese sauce, and spoon mixture onto crepes. Fold, and place in greased baking dish. Pour remaining sauce over crepes and sprinkle with grated cheese. Bake at 350° F. (177° C.) until hot. Broil to brown cheese. Garnish with pimiento strips.

Makes 8 individual servings.
SUGGESTED CREPE BATTER: ENTREE II
SUGGESTED CREPE FOLD: TRADITIONAL

CABBAGE STRUDEL CREPES

2 cups (480 ml) shredded cabbage
1/4 cup (60 ml) finely
  chopped onion
2 tablespoons (30 ml) butter
  or margarine
1/2 teaspoon (2.5 ml) salt

Dash pepper
2 tablespoons (30 ml) dry
  bread crumbs
Butter or margarine
  for frying

8 crepes

Saute cabbage and onion in butter until tender. Add remaining ingredients and mix well. Spoon onto crepes and fold for frying. Let stand, uncovered, 30 minutes to dry crepes slightly. Melt butter in frypan. Fry filled crepes until brown on both sides.

Makes 8 individual servings.
SUGGESTED CREPE BATTER: ENTREE I
SUGGESTED CREPE FOLD: FRY FOLD

CARROTS IN CHEESE SAUCE

1/3 cup (80 ml) butter
    or margarine
2 tablespoons (30 ml) heavy cream
1 cup (240 ml) Parmesan cheese
1/4 teaspoon (5 ml) basil

1/4 teaspoon (1.5 ml) thyme
Salt and pepper
2 cups (480 ml) sliced
    carrots, cooked

6 crepes

Melt butter in saucepan. Add cream and Parmesan cheese and stir over low heat until melted. Stir in seasonings. Reserve 1/3 cup sauce. Add carrots to remaining sauce and spoon onto crepes. Fold and place in greased baking dish. Pour remaining sauce over crepes and sprinkle with additional Parmesan cheese. Bake at 350° F. (177° C.) until hot and lightly browned.

Makes 6 individual servings.
SUGGESTED CREPE BATTER: ENTREE II
SUGGESTED CREPE FOLD: TRADITIONAL

CHEDDAR PLUS SANDWICHES

1 cup (240 ml) grated sharp
    Cheddar cheese
2 tablespoons (30 ml) finely
    chopped celery
1 tablespoon (15 ml) chopped
    pimiento-stuffed olives

1 teaspoon (5 ml) Dijon-style mustard
1/4 teaspoon (1.5 ml) chili powder
2 tablespoons (30 ml) mayonnaise
8 slices salami, bologna or ham

4 crepes

Toss together cheese, celery and olives. Stir in mustard, chili powder and mayonnaise. Lay two meat slices on each crepe. Spoon cheese mixture in strip down center. Roll crepe and serve. Garnish with pimiento-stuffed olives.

Makes 4 individual servings.
SUGGESTED CREPE BATTER: ENTREE II
SUGGESTED CREPE FOLD: SPIRAL ROLL

CHEESE BLINTZES DEVINE

1-1/2 pounds (680 g) farmers
    cheese or very dry
    cottage cheese
2 egg yolks, beaten

Salt and pepper
3 tablespoons (45 ml) butter
Sour cream or apple sauce
4 teaspoons (20 ml) sugar

8 crepes

Mash cheese with fork. Add egg yolks and sugar. Add salt and pepper to taste. Spoon about 4 tablespoons onto each crepe. Fold for frying. Let crepes stand uncovered about 30 minutes until dried slightly. Melt butter in frypan. Fry filled crepes until brown on both sides. Serve with sour cream or apple sauce.

Makes 4 servings of 2 blintzes each.
SUGGESTED CREPE BATTER: ENTREE II
SUGGESTED CREPE FOLD: FRY

CHEESE CREPES PROVENCAL

4 slices bacon, crumbled
1 cup (240 ml) Swiss cheese
2 tablespoons (30 ml) flour
1/4 teaspoon (1.5 ml) salt

1/4 teaspoon (1.5 ml) pepper
Dash of cayenne
1/2 teaspoon (2.5 ml)
    powdered mustard

12 crepes

Cook bacon until crisp. Drain and crumble. Line greased muffin pans or individual custard cups with crepes, flute and trim to fit. Sprinkle bacon in crepe shells. Top with cheese. Beat flour, salt, pepper, cayenne and mustard together and pour over cheese. Bake in preheated oven at 350° F. (177° C.) for 15 to 20 minutes, or until firm. Cook about 5 minutes before removing from pan. Garnish with parsley.

Makes 12 individual crepes.
SUGGESTED CREPE BATTER: ENTREE II
SUGGESTED CREPE FOLD: BASKET

CREAMY ZUCCHINI CREPES

2 zucchini, diced
1 tablespoon (15 ml) butter
    or margarine
2 tablespoons (30 ml) chopped
    scallion

1/2 teaspoon (2.5 ml) salt
1/4 teaspoon (1.5 ml) pepper
1-1/2 ounce (45 g) cream cheese
1 cup (240 ml) sour cream
Paprika

6 crepes

In frypan, saute zucchini in butter until just tender. Add scallion, salt and pepper. Cut cream cheese into 6 strips. Spoon zucchini and 1 piece cream cheese onto each crepe. Fold and place in greased baking dish. Bake at 350° F. (177° C.) for 10 minutes, or until cheese melts. Remove, spoon sour cream over top. Sprinkle with paprika and bake another 1-2 minutes to heat sour cream. To prevent curdling, do not overcook sour cream. Serve immediately, garnished with raw zucchini strips and cherry tomatoes.

Makes 6 individual servings.
SUGGESTED CREPE BATTER: ENTREE II
SUGGESTED CREPE FOLD: TRADITIONAL

CREPES A L'A WALDORF

1 tablespoon (15 ml) lemon juice
1/4 cup (60 ml) mayonnaise
3 medium apples, cored and diced
1/2 cup (120 ml) sliced celery

1/4 cup (60 ml) chopped walnuts
1 teaspoon (5 ml) sugar
1/2 teaspoon (2.5 ml) salt
6 leaves lettuce

6 crepes

Blend lemon juice into mayonnaise. Combine the apples, celery, walnuts, mayonnaise, sugar and salt. Place lettuce leaf in each crepe. Top with apple mixture. Fold, and fasten with toothpick.

Makes 6 individual servings.
SUGGESTED CREPE BATTER: NUTTY
SUGGESTED CREPE FOLD: SPIRAL ROLL

DIVINE CHEESE CREPES

1/2 cup (120 ml) grated
   Swiss cheese
2 3-ounce package (170 g)
   cream cheese
1/2 cup (120 ml) cottage cheese
2 tablespoons (30 ml) butter
   or margarine
1 small clove garlic, crushed

Dash paprika
1 or 2 drops bottled hot pepper sauce
2 tablespoons (30 ml) dry vermouth
   or dry white wine
1 egg, slightly beaten
Oil for frying

8 crepes

Combine Swiss cheese, cream cheese and cottage cheese, butter, garlic, paprika, hot pepper sauce and wine in top of double boiler. Heat, stirring constantly, over slowly boiling water until mixture is smooth—about 5 minutes. Spoon mixture into crepes. Fold. Dip crepes into beaten egg and fry in 1 inch oil at 375° F. (190° C.) until browned on both sides. Drain on paper towels. Garnish with parsley and cherry tomatoes.

Makes 4 servings of 2 crepes each.
SUGGESTED CREPE BATTER: ENTREE II
SUGGESTED CREPE FOLD: FRY

EASY SPINACH SOUFFLE CREPES

12-ounce package (340 g) frozen spinach souffle

4 crepes

Bake spinach souffle as directed. Divide into 4 long strips with a knife. Transfer each section to a crepe, fold, and place crepes in greased baking dish. Bake at 350° F. (177° C.) for 10 minutes to crisp crepes.

Makes 4 individual servings.
SUGGESTED CREPE BATTER: ENTREE II
SUGGESTED CREPE FOLD: TRADITIONAL

"GARDEN GREENS" CREPES

2 cups (480 ml) shredded cabbage
1 cup (240 ml) thinly sliced celery
1/2 green pepper, thinly sliced
1/4 cup (60 ml) chopped onion
1/4 cup (60 ml) sliced
    mushrooms (optional)
1/4 cup (60 ml) butter
    or margarine

1 tablespoon (15 ml) sugar
1 tablespoon (15 ml) lemon juice
1/4 teaspoon (1.5 ml) salt
1/8 teaspoon (1 ml) pepper
1/2 teaspoon (2.5 ml) soy sauce
2 tablespoons (30 ml) sliced pimiento

8 crepes

Cook cabbage, celery, green pepper, onion and mushrooms in butter in frypan over medium heat until vegetables are crisp-tender, about 5 minutes. Stir in sugar, lemon juice, salt, pepper, soy sauce and pimiento. Spoon vegetable mixture onto center of crepe. Top with Mock Hollandaise Sauce.

Makes 8 individual servings.
SUGGESTED CREPE BATTER: ENTREE I
SUGGESTED CREPE FOLD: TRADITIONAL

GREEK SPINACH AND CHEESE CREPES

2 10-ounce boxes (570 g) frozen
    spinach, thawed
1 medium onion, finely chopped
2 tablespoons (30 ml) olive oil
1/2 pound (225 g) feta cheese
4 eggs, beaten

1/4 cup (60 ml) fresh
    chopped parsley
1/2 teaspoon (2.5 ml) dill weed
1/2 teaspoon (2.5 ml) salt
Dash black pepper
Dash nutmeg

8 to 10 crepes

Thoroughly drain spinach. In frypan, saute spinach and onion in olive oil until tender, about 5 minutes. Remove from heat and add all remaining ingredients; mix well. Spoon mixture onto crepes. Fold and place in lightly greased baking dish. Bake at 350° F. (177° C.) for 25-30 minutes, or until hot.

For an Italian version, substitute ricotta cheese for the feta and add 1/2 cup Parmesan cheese and 1 cup finely diced cooked smoked pork.

Makes 8 to 10 individual crepes.
SUGGESTED CREPE BATTER: ENTREE I
SUGGESTED CREPE FOLD: TRADITIONAL

GREEN BEANS BECHAMEL

1 tablespoon (15 ml) butter
   or margarine
1/2 cup (120 ml) slivered almonds
1-1/2 cups (360 ml) Bechamel Sauce

2 cups (480 ml) cut green
   beans, cooked
3 tablespoons (45 ml)
   grated Parmesan cheese

6 crepes

Melt butter in electric frypan. Add almonds and stir over medium heat until browned. Add about half the Bechamel Sauce and the beans. Stir. Spoon onto crepes, fold, and place in greased baking dish. Pour remaining sauce over crepes and sprinkle with Parmesan cheese. Bake at 350° F. (177° C.) for 10-15 minutes, or until hot, bubbly and lightly browned. Top with slivered almonds.

Makes 6 individual crepes.
SUGGESTED CREPE BATTER: ENTREE II
SUGGESTED CREPE FOLD: TRADITIONAL

LATE SUPPER CREPES

8 eggs
4 tablespoons (60 ml) milk or water
2 tablespoons (30 ml) chopped parsley
1 tablespoon (15 ml) finely chopped
   chives or scallion
2 tablespoons (30 ml) finely chopped
   green pepper
1 teaspoon (5 ml) dill weed

1/2 teaspoon (2.5 ml) salt
1/4 teaspoon (1.5 ml) dry mustard
1/4 teaspoon (1.5 ml) pepper
Dash garlic salt
2 tablespoons (30 ml) butter
   or margarine
1 cup (240 ml) alfalfa sprouts
2 cups (480 ml) Cheese Sauce

8 crepes

Beat eggs until thick and lemon colored. Add milk, parsley, scallion, green pepper and seasonings. Melt butter in electric frypan. Add eggs and scramble gently. Spoon eggs and alfalfa sprouts into crepes, fold, and place on serving platter. Pour Cheese Sauce over crepes. Garnish with green pepper rings.

Makes 8 individual servings.
SUGGESTED CREPE BATTER: ENTREE II
SUGGESTED CREPE FOLD: TRADITIONAL

MANDARIN VEGETABLE CREPES

1 cup (240 ml) thinly sliced carrots
1 cup (240 ml) green beans,
   cut into 1-inch pieces
1 tablespoon (15 ml) sesame oil
3/4 cup (180 ml) thinly
   sliced cauliflower

1/2 cup (120 ml) chicken broth
2 teaspoons (10 ml) soy sauce
1-1/2 teaspoons (7.5 ml) cornstarch
1/3 cup (80 ml) sliced scallion
1/3 cup (80 ml) slivered almonds

8 crepes

Saute carrots and green beans in oil for 2 minutes. Add cauliflower, cover and simmer 2 minutes longer. Combine chicken broth, soy sauce and cornstarch. Add to vegetables and simmer, covered, until just tender. Add scallion and almonds. Spoon mixutre onto crepes and fold. Serve immediately, garnished with mandarin orange slices.

Makes 8 individual servings.
SUGGESTED CREPE BATTER: ENTREE I
SUGGESTED CREPE FOLD: TRADITIONAL

MUSHROOM CREPES

1 pound (455 g) fresh
   mushrooms, sliced
1 single serving package
   onion soup mix

2 tablespoons (30 ml) parsley,
   chopped
1/2 cup (120 ml) sherry
   or Madeira wine

8 crepes

Wash and slice mushrooms. In saucepan, prepare soup mix as directed, add mushrooms and simmer until soft, about 15 to 20 minutes. Add parsley and wine, cover and simmer 5 to 10 minutes more. Spoon mixture onto crepes, fold, place in greased baking pan and bake at 375° F. (190° C.) for 10 to 15 minutes. Garnish with raw mushroom slices and parsley sprigs.

Makes 8 individual servings.
SUGGESTED CREPE BATTER: ENTREE I
SUGGESTED CREPE FOLD: TRADITIONAL

NUTTY SQUASH CREPES

1-1/2 cups (360 ml) finely diced,
   cooked acorn or
   butternut squash
1/4 cup (60 ml) maple sugar

2 tablespoons (30 ml) butter
   or margarine
1/2 cup (120 ml) chopped peanuts
Salt and pepper

6 crepes

Combine squash, maple syrup and butter. Heat, stirring frequently. Stir in peanuts. Season to taste with salt and pepper. Spoon onto crepes and fold. Serve immediately.

Makes 6 individual servings.
SUGGESTED CREPE BATTER: ENTREE II
SUGGESTED CREPE FOLD: TRADITIONAL

PEPPERONI-CHICK PEA CREPES

1-1/2 cups (360 ml) pepperoni
    sausage, sliced thin
1 medium onion
1 small green pepper, chopped
1 clove garlic, crushed
2 tablespoons (30 ml) margarine
8-ounce can (225 g) tomato sauce
2 tablespoons (30 ml) dry white wine

1/2 teaspoon (2.5 ml) oregano
1/4 teaspoon (1.5 ml) basil
1 tablespoon (15 ml) brown sugar
20-ounce can (570 g) chick
    peas, drained
4-ounce (115 g) Cheddar
    cheese, grated

8 crepes

Fry pepperoni; remove from frypan. Saute onion, green pepper and garlic in 2 tablespoons margarine. Add tomato sauce, wine, oregano, basil and brown sugar. Simmer 20 minutes. Add pepperoni and chick peas. Spoon onto crepes. Fold, and place in baking dish. Sprinkle with Cheddar cheese. Bake in 350° F. (177° C.) oven until cheese is browned. Garnish with pimiento and green pepper strips.

Makes 8 individual servings.
SUGGESTED CREPE BATTER: ENTREE
SUGGESTED CREPE FOLD: TRADITIONAL

POTATO BLINTZES, JEWISH STYLE

1/4 cup (60 ml) finely minced onion
1 tablespoon (15 ml) butter
    or margarine
2 cups (480 ml) cooked
    mashed potatoes

1 egg, beaten
1/4 teaspoon (1.5 ml) salt
Dash pepper
Dash paprika
Butter or margarine for frying

8 to 10 crepes

In frypan, saute onion in butter until tender. Add potatoes, egg and seasonings. Spoon about 3 to 3-1/2 tablespoons into each crepe; fold for frying. Let stand, uncovered, 30 minutes to dry crepes slightly. Melt butter in frypan and fry filled crepes until brown on both sides.

Serve hot with sour cream sprinkled with chives.
Makes 8-10 individual servings.
SUGGESTED CREPE BATTER: ENTREE II
SUGGESTED CREPE FOLD: FRY OR POCKET FOLD

RATATOUILLE CREPES

1 green pepper, cut into strips
1 medium onion, sliced
1 clove garlic, crushed
2 tablespoons (30 ml) olive oil
2 cups (480 ml) sliced zucchini
1 cup (240 ml) peeled, seeded,
    quartered tomatoes
1 cup (240 ml) diced eggplant

3/4 teaspoons (3.5 ml) salt
1/2 teaspoon (2.5 ml) basil
1/4 teaspoon (1.5 ml) oregano
Dash pepper
1 tablespoon (15 ml) cornstarch
1 tablespoon (15 ml) water
1/4 cup (60 ml) Parmesan cheese

8 crepes

In saucepan, saute green pepper, onion and garlic in olive oil until tender. Add zucchini, tomatoes, egg plant and seasonings. Cover and cook over low heat 20-30 minutes until done. Occasionally stir gently. Remove from heat. Combine cornstarch and water and gradually stir into vegetables. Cook until thickened. Spoon onto crepes, fold, and place in greased baking dish. Sprinkle with Parmesan cheese and broil until crepes are brown on edges and cheese is crisp. Sprinkle with chopped parsley.

Makes 8 individual servings.
SUGGESTED CREPE BATTER: ENTREE I
SUGGESTED CREPE FOLD: TRADITIONAL

SPICY CHEDDAR CREPES

1/4 pound (115 g) sliced bacon
1 small onion, finely chopped
1/2 pound (225 g)
    sliced mushrooms
1/3 cup (80 ml) green pepper,
    chopped

8 ounces (225 g) grated
    Cheddar cheese
2 teaspoons (10 ml)
    Worchestershire sauce
2 or 3 drops bottled hot
    pepper sauce

8 crepes

Fry bacon until crisp. Remove from frypan and drain. Saute onion, mushrooms and green pepper in 2 tablespoons of bacon drippings. Remove from heat. Set aside about one-quarter of the cheese. Add remaining cheese, Worcestershire and hot pepper sauce to vegetables. Crumble bacon and add to mixture. Toss lightly. Spoon mixture onto crepes. Fold, and place in greased baking dish. Pour tomato sauce over crepes, sprinkle with reserved cheese and bake at 375° F. (190° C.) for 15 to 20 minutes, or until cheese is melted. Garnish with sweet pickle chips.

Makes 4 servings of 2 crepes each.
SUGGESTED CREPE BATTER: ENTREE II
SUGGESTED CREPE FOLD: TRADITIONAL

SPINACH CHEESE CREPES

10-ounce package (285 g)
   frozen chopped spinach
5 slices bacon
1 cup (240 ml) creamed cottage
   cheese
2 tablespoons (30 ml) minced onion

1/4 teaspoon (1.5 ml) pepper
2 tablespoons (30 ml) soy sauce
2 4-ounce cans (225 g) water
   chestnuts, sliced
1/2 cup (120 ml) Mozzarella
   cheese, grated

6 to 8 crepes

Cook spinach as directed on package. Drain thoroughly. In frypan, prepare bacon. Drain grease. Crumble bacon, set aside. Place spinach in frypan, fold in cottage cheese, bacon, onion, pepper, soy sauce and water chestnuts. Heat thoroughly. Place 1 tablespoon Mozzarella on crepe. Spoon spinach mixture onto crepe. Fold; sprinkle remaining cheese on top. Place crepes in greased baking dish and bake at 350° F. (177° C.) until cheese melts, about 5 minutes. Garnish with thin slices of lemon brushed with paprika.

Makes 6 to 8 individual servings.
SUGGESTED CREPE BATTER: ENTREE I
SUGGESTED CREPE FOLD: TRADITONAL

SPINACH CREPES

10-ounce package (285 g) frozen
   chopped spinach
1-3/4 cups (420 ml)
   Mornay Sauce

1/8 teaspoon (1 ml) nutmeg
Salt and pepper
2 tablespoons (30 ml)
   Parmesan cheese

8 crepes

Cook spinach according to package directions. Drain well. Add 3/4 cup Mornay Sauce and nutmeg. Season to taste with salt and pepper. Spoon mixture onto crepes, fold, and place in greased baking dish. Pour remaining sauce over crepes, sprinkle with Parmesan cheese. Bake at 350° F. (177° C.) until sauce bubbles. Garnish with rounds of hard-cooked egg and pimiento.

Makes 6 to 8 individual servings.
SUGGESTED CREPE BATTER: ENTREE I
SUGGESTED CREPE FOLD: TRADITIONAL

SPINACH SPECIALS

2 medium onions, thinly sliced
2 cloves garlic, minced
2 tablespoons (30 ml) oil
2 medium tomatoes, peeled
    and chopped

2 cups (480 ml) spinach,
    cooked and drained
1/2 cup (120 ml) mushrooms,
    sliced
Salt and pepper to taste
1/4 teaspoon (1.5 ml) rosemary
1 cup (240 ml) Cheddar
    cheese, grated

8 crepes

In frypan, saute onion and garlic slowly in oil until tender. Add tomato, spinach, mushrooms, salt and pepper and rosemary. Heat thoroughly. Place about 4 tablespoons of spinach mixture on each crepe. Sprinkle with cheese. Fold. Garnish with thin rounds of lemon.

Makes 8 individual servings.
SUGGESTED CREPE BATTER: ENTREE II
SUGGESTED CREPE FOLD: TRADITIONAL

SWEET-AND-SOUR CABBAGE CREPES

16-ounce can (455 g) sauerkraut,
    drained
3 tablespoons (45 ml) butter
    or margraine
1/2 cup (120 ml) brown sugar

1/3 cup (80 ml) lemon juice
Salt and pepper
2 tablespoons (30 ml) butter
    or margarine

8 crepes

Thoroughly drain sauerkraut. In frypan, saute drained sauerkraut in 3 tablespoons butter until well browned. Add brown sugar and lemon juice; season to taste with salt and pepper. Spoon sauerkraut and about 3/4 teaspoons cream cheese into each crepe; fold for frying. Let stand, uncovered, 30 minutes to dry crepes slightly. Melt 2 tablespoons butter in electric frypan. Fry filled crepes on both sides until brown.

Makes 8 individual servings.
SUGGESTED CREPE BATTER: ENTREE I
SUGGESTED CREPE FOLD: FRY FOLD

TOMATO-OKRA COMBO

10-ounce package (285 g) cut
   frozen okra
1/4 cup (60 ml) chopped celery
1/2 cup (120 ml) sliced onion
1/3 cup (80 ml) chopped
   green pepper
1 tablespoon (15 ml) oil
1 bay leaf
Pinch of leaf oregano

1 teaspoon (5 ml) salt
1/4 teaspoon (1.5 ml) pepper
1/2 teaspoon (2.5 ml) Worcestershire
   sauce
3 whole tomatoes, or 1 cup (240 ml)
canned tomatoes
1 tablespoon (15 ml) cornstarch
1/3 cup (80 ml) tomato juice

8 crepes

Cook frozen okra according to package directions; drain. In frypan, saute celery, onion, green pepper in oil until tender. Add seasonings, Worcestershire sauce, tomatoes, and okra. Blend cornstarch with tomato juice and add to vegetable mixture. Cook until mixture thickens—about 20 minutes. Spoon mixture onto crepes, and fold.

Makes 8 individual servings.
SUGGESTED CREPE BATTER: ENTREE I
SUGGESTED CREPE FOLD: TRADITIONAL

VEGETABLE CREOLE CREPES

2 tablespoons (30 ml) margarine
1/2 cup (120 ml) chopped onion
1/4 cup (60 ml) green pepper
1/2 cup (120 ml) diced celery
1/2 clove garlic, minced
1 cup (240 ml) water
1-pound can (455 g) tomatoes
1/2 bay leaf
1/8 teaspoon (1 ml) leaf thyme

1 tablespoon (15 ml) chopped parsley
1/2 teaspoon (2.5 ml) salt
1/4 teaspoon (1.5 ml) pepper
1 teaspoon (5 ml) chili powder
1/2 cup (120 ml) long
   grain rice, uncooked
1/2 cup (120 ml) cooked green
   beans, chopped

8 crepes

Melt margarine in large frypan. Saute onion, green pepper and celery. Combine all remaining ingredients. Simmer until rice is tender, 20 to 30 minutes. Spoon mixture onto crepes. Fold. Garnish with additional mixture and parsley.

Makes 8 individual crepes.
SUGGESTED CREPE BATTER: ENTREE II
SUGGESTED CREPE FOLD: TRADITIONAL

VEGETABLE SALAD VINAIGRETTE

2 8-ounce cans (455 g) mixed
   beans for salad, drained
1 large onion, thinly sliced
1 cup (240 ml) chopped celery
1/2 cup (120 ml) olive or
   salad oil

1/3 cup (80 ml) red wine vinegar
1 teaspoon thyme leaves,
   crumbled
Salt and pepper
8 slices salami, cut
   in strips

8 crepes

In a medium bowl, mix beans, onion and chopped celery with oil and vinegar. Add seasonings and toss. Refrigerate. To serve, drain excess dressing. Spoon mixture onto crepes. Top with salami. Fold. Garnish with pimiento and olive slices.

Makes 8 to 10 individual crepes.
SUGGESTED CREPE BATTER: ENTREE I
SUGGESTED CREPE FOLD: TRADITIONAL

ZUCCHINI CREPES

1 medium onion
1 clove garlic, minced
1 stalk celery, chopped fine
1/2 medium green pepper
6 small zucchini squash, diced
2 tablespoons (30 ml) olive oil

1/4 teaspoon (1.5 ml) crushed oregano
1 tablespoon (15 ml) Parmesan
   cheese, grated
1/8 teaspoon (1 ml) pepper
1 recipe Marinara Sauce

8 crepes

In frypan, saute onion, garlic, celery, green pepper and zucchini in olive oil. Mix Parmesan cheese, pepper and oregano with sauteed vegetables. Spoon onto crepes. Fold. Top with heated Marinara Sauce. Garnish with green pepper rings.

Makes 8 individual servings.
SUGGESTED CREPE BATTER: ENTREE I
SUGGESTED CREPE FOLD: SPIRAL

DESSERTS

Almendrado
Apple Raisin Crepes
Baked Alaska Crepes
Banana-Coconut Cream Crepes
Banana Delight Crepes
Beignets
Candied Fruit Torte
Cannoli
Caramel Custard Crepes
Cheese Blintzes
Cherries Jubilee Crepes
Cherry A La Mode Crepes
Chocolate-Mocha Crepes
Chocolate Mousse
Choc-O-Mint
Choc-O-Nut
Chocolate Velvet Dessert
Cinnamon-Nut Cookies
Coconut Nibbles
Coconut S'Mores
Creamy Lemon Crepes
Crepes A La Mode
Crepes Chantilly
Crepes in
    Flaming Wine Sauce
Crepes Suzette
Crispy Coconut Cookies
Date-Nut Cookies

Easy Lemon Crepes
Flaming Apricot-Nut Crepes
Flaming Banana Crepes
Flaming Coffee
    Liqueur Crepes
Fluffy Cream Cheese Crepes
French Silk Crepes
Fruity Custard Crepes
Fruity Pudding Crepes
Hellenic Honey Nut Roll
Irish Coffee Crepes
Key Lime Crepes
Lemon-Grape Crepes
Oriental Pineapple-Rice Dessert
Peach Melba Crepes
Peach Supreme Crepes
Peppermint Crepes
Poires Bourdaloue Crepes
Polynesian Fruit Crepes
Rhubarb-Strawberry Crepes
Rice Pudding Chiffon Crepes
Sour Cream-Raisin Crepes
Southern Pecan Roll
Spicy Fruit Crepes
Swedish Pancakes
Tropical Magic Crepes
Yogurt Crepes

FINISHING WITH A FLAIR . . . DESSERTS

Did you know that the word dessert comes from the French verb *desservir*, which means to clear or take away? It was so named because the table was cleared completely after dinner and then set up again, offering a complete buffet of fruit and sweets.

No wonder the French, again, developed the most famous crepe dessert in the world, *Crepes Suzette*. Who was Suzette? No one knows for sure, but the stories of the dessert's origin are many. Numerous, too, are the other crepe desserts which have been developed over the years.

The most glorious of these concoctions are served flaming. If you've tried this and agonized because the flames went out before the dessert was served, keep these few simple techniques in mind.

Heat the liqueur before lighting. However, the higher the proof, the lower the liqueur's temperature needs to be when ignited. A low-proof liqueur should be very hot, while a high-proof liqueur need only be warm. Never boil liqueurs. Avoid using liqueurs lower than 35 proof; they are difficult to ignite.

Be sure there are no combustible materials nearby when lighting the crepes. Use a long fireplace match to light the flame; this ensures safety, and also is more attractive than an ordinary match.

Baste crepes only after flames have died down.

Be sure all flames are extinguished before serving.

Remember, you can flambe your crepes in any skillet or shallow wide-bottom pan, including a chafing dish, as well as in the traditional crepe finishing pan.

No matter how you serve the crepes, you'll be adding a gourmet touch to your meal. No one need ever know how simple they are to make.

ALMENDRADO

---

1 envelope unflavored gelatin	1/4 teaspoon (1.5 ml)
1/4 cup (60 ml) cold water	almond extract
5 egg whites	1/4 teaspoon (1.5 ml) grated lemon peel
3/4 cup (180 ml) sugar	Red and green food coloring
	Almond Custard Sauce

6 crepes

Soften gelatin in cold water. Dissolve over hot water. Separate eggs. Reserve egg yolks for Almond Custard Sauce. In large mixing bowl, mix egg whites. Add gelatin. Beat egg whites at high speed until a thick white foam is formed. Continue beating at high speed, gradually adding sugar, 1 tablespoon at a time—about 1 minute. Add almond extract and lemon peel. Tint 1/3 of the meringue pink and 1/3 green. Place meringue in a shallow dish. Chill for 2 to 6 hours. To serve, place crepe flat on serving platter, top with 1/2 green tinted almendrado. Place another crepe on top. Top with 1/2 white almendrado and place another crepe on top. Top with 1/2 pink almendrado. The layers should be alternated, ending with the pink layer on top. Top with Almond Custard Sauce. Cut into wedges to serve.

Makes 6 individual servings.

SUGGESTED CREPE BATTER: BASIC DESSERT
SUGGESTED CREPE FOLD: LAYER

APPLE RAISIN CREPES

3 tablespoons (45 ml) margarine
5 tart cooking apples, peeled,
    cored and thinly sliced
1/4 cup (60 ml) brown sugar

1/2 cup (120 ml) raisins
1/2 teaspoon (2.5 ml) cinnamon
1 teaspoon (5 ml) lemon juice
1/2 cup (120 ml) whipped cream

6 crepes

Melt margarine in frying pan. Add apple slices, brown sugar, raisins, and cinnamon. Heat thoroughly. Add lemon juice. Spoon mixture onto crepe, and fold. Serve topped with whipped cream.

Makes 4 individual servings.
SUGGESTED CREPE BATTER: BASIC DESSERT
SUGGESTED CREPE FOLD: TRADITIONAL

BAKED ALASKA CREPES

1/2 gallon (2.5 l) ice cream
8 egg whites

1/2 cup (120 ml) sugar

8 crepes

Cut ice cream into logs 5 inches long and 1 inch in diameter. Place in freezer on cookie sheet while preparing meringue. For meringue, beat egg whites on highest speed of electric mixer until foamy. Gradually add sugar, continuing beating until stiff peaks are formed. Cut a piece of heavy brown paper to fit cookie sheet. Place an ice cream log on crepe. Fold. Place on cookie sheet. Spread meringue over top and down sides of crepe, sealing crepe around the bottom where it meets the brown paper. Place in the freezer overnight. Preheat oven to 500° F (260°C.) Place frozen crepe in oven and bake 3 minutes, or until meringue is golden brown. Remove and serve at once, garnished with candied fruit.

Makes 8 individual servings.
SUGGESTED CREPE BATTER: BASIC DESSERT
SUGGESTED CREPE FOLD: SPIRAL ROLL

BANANA-COCONUT CREAM CREPES

3-1/2-ounce package (100 g) coconut
    cream pudding/pie filling mix
1 cup (240 ml) heavy cream
2 teaspoons (10 ml) lemon juice

2 small bananas, sliced
1/2 cup (120 ml) toasted
    coconut or chopped nuts

4 crepes

Prepare coconut cream pudding according to package directions, reducing milk to 1-1/2 cups. Cool. Beat 1/2 cup cream until it forms soft peaks. Fold into pudding. Toss lemon juice with bananas to prevent darkening, drain, and fold into pudding. Chill. Spoon pudding onto crepes; fold. Top with remaining heavy cream, whipped and sweetened to taste. Sprinkle with toasted coconut or chopped nuts.

Makes 4 individual crepes.
SUGGESTED CREPE BATTER: DESSERT
SUGGESTED CREPE FOLD: TRADITIONAL

BANANA DELIGHT CREPES

3 large bananas, sliced
2 teaspoons (10 ml) lemon juice
1/3 cup (80 ml) margarine
1/2 cup (60 ml) orange marmalade

2 tablespoons (30 ml) sugar
1 tablespoon (15 ml) cornstarch
Sour cream
Ground nutmeg (optional)

8 crepes

Slice bananas and toss with lemon juice to prevent the bananas from turning brown. In frypan, melt margarine and orange marmalade, stirring constantly. Mix the sugar and the cornstarch together; slowly stir into the margarine and marmalade mixture until bubbly and smooth. Remove from heat. Fold in sliced bananas. Spoon mixture onto center of crepe; fold. Top crepe with sour cream, sprinkle with nutmeg.

Makes 8 individual servings.
SUGGESTED CREPE BATTER: BASIC DESSERT
SUGGESTED CREPE FOLD: TRADITIONAL

BEIGNETS

Cut Cinnamon-Nut Dessert Crepes into 8 pie-shape wedges. Fry in 3/4 inch hot (375°F.) (190°C.) oil until edges begin to turn brown. Turn once. Drain on paper towels. While still warm, sprinkle with confectioner's sugar. Serve warm or cold with Brandied Apricot Sauce or Mocha Sauce. Allow 1 or 2 crepes per person.

CANDIED FRUIT TORTE

1 cup (240 ml) heavy cream
1/2 cup (120 ml) finely-chopped,
    candied fruits (red cherries,
    green cherries, pineapple,
    citron, orange peel)
1/4 cup (60 ml)
    finely-chopped pecans

2 tablespoons (30 ml)
    confectioner's sugar
1/2 cup (120 ml) whole
    candied red cherries
1/4 cup (60 ml) pecan halves

6 crepes

Beat cream until it forms soft peaks. Fold in chopped fruit and nuts. Sweeten to taste with confectioner's sugar. Spread one crepe with about 1/3 cup fruit mixture; lay another crepe on top. Repeat, alternating layers of crepes and filling, using six layers of each. Cut whole cherries in half, place cherry and pecan halves around outside of top layer. Chill at least 1-1/2 hours before serving. To serve, cut in pie-shape wedges.

Makes 8-12 servings.
SUGGESTED CREPE BATTER: DESSERT
SUGGESTED CREPE FOLD: LAYER

CANNOLI

2 cups (480 ml) ricotta cheese
3/4 cup (180 ml) sugar
2 teaspoons (10 ml)
   vanilla extract

1/4 cup (60 ml) citron
   and orange peel
2 tablespoons (30 ml)
   chopped milk chocolate

4 crepes

Blend ricotta cheese in blender until very smooth. Add sugar and vanilla to cheese and combine. Mix in chopped fruit and chocolate. Remove from blender jar. Fill crepe with 2 tablespoons of mixture, fold, and freeze. Cut into 3 pieces and top with sifted confectioner's sugar.

Makes 12 individual servings.
SUGGESTED CREPE BATTER: CHOCOLATE OR BASIC DESSERT
SUGGESTED CREPE FOLD: SPIRAL ROLL

CARAMEL CUSTARD CREPES

Caramel:

3/4 cup (180 ml) sugar

3/4 cup (180 ml) boiling water

Custard:

2 cups (480 ml) milk, scalded
1/4 cup (60 ml) sugar
1/2 teaspoon (2.5 ml) vanilla

Dash salt
2 eggs beaten

4 crepes
Caramel

Melt sugar in electric frypan, stirring constantly. When sugar is light golden brown, remove from heat and gradually stir in water. (Sugar may become hard, but will melt again when heated). Boil caramel slowly for 5 minutes. Chill to thicken.

Custard

Combine milk with sugar and salt; cool slightly. Gradually add mixture to beaten eggs. Stir in vanilla. Pour into 1-1/2-quart casserole and set in pan of hot water. Bake at 350° F. (177° C.) for 45-50 minutes, or until knife inserted about 1 inch from edge comes out clean. Cool. Chill 3 to 4 hours.

Spoon custard into 6 crepes. Fold, and spoon chilled caramel sauce over crepes.

Makes 4 individual servings.
SUGGESTED CREPE BATTER: DESSERT
SUGGESTED CREPE FOLD: TRADITIONAL

CHEESE BLINTZES

1 cup (240 ml) ricotta cheese
2/3 cup (360 ml) cottage cheese
1/2 cup (60 ml)
　confectioner's sugar
1/2 teaspoon (2.5 ml) vanilla

1/2 teaspoon (2.5 ml)
　grated lemon peel
1/2 cup (60 ml) butter, melted
Strawberry preserves

6 crepes

Combine ricotta, cottage cheese, sugar, vanilla and lemon peel. Spoon onto crepe. Fold and place in greased 8 x 6 x 2-inch baking dish. Keep warm in moderate oven. To serve, spread with melted butter and sprinkle with powdered sugar. Top with strawberry preserves.

Makes 6 individual servings.
SUGGESTED CREPE BATTER: BASIC DESSERT
SUGGESTED CREPE FOLD: TRADITIONAL

CHERRIES JUBILEE CREPES

16-ounce can (455 g) pitted,
　dark, sweet cherries
2 tablespoons (30 ml) cornstarch

1-1/2 pints (600 ml)
　vanilla ice cream
1/2 cup (60 ml) brandy

6 crepes

Combine juice from cherries with cornstarch; set aside. Melt jelly in saucepan over low heat. Add cherry juice mixture and stir constantly until thickened. Add cherries. Pour sauce into chafing dish. Spoon ice cream into center of crepes, and fold. Heat brandy to lukewarm, ignite and pour over cherry sauce. Allow flames to burn out, spoon sauce over crepes and serve.

Makes 6 individual servings.
SUGGESTED CREPE BATTER: DESSERT
SUGGESTED CREPE FOLD: TRADITIONAL

CHERRY A LA MODE CREPES

16-ounce can (455 g)
　cherry pie filling
Dash cinnamon
1 teaspoon (5 ml) brandy

1-1/2 pints (600 ml)
　vanilla ice cream
1/2 cup (120 ml) toasted
　slivered almonds

8 crepes

Combine cherry pie filling, cinnamon and brandy. Spoon onto crepes and fold. Top with ice cream and slivered almonds.

Makes 8 individual servings.
SUGGESTED CREPE BATTER: DESSERT
SUGGESTED CREPE FOLD: TRADITIONAL

CHOCOLATE-MOCHA CREPES

1/4 cup (60 ml) cocoa
1/2 cup (120 ml) maple syrup
1 teaspoon (5 ml)
   freeze-dried coffee

1/4 teaspoon (1.5 ml) vanilla
3 5-ounce cans (425 g)
   chocolate pudding
1 recipe Sweetened Whipped Cream

6 crepes

Sift cocoa into small saucepan. Stir in 1/4 cup maple syrup to make smooth paste. Add remaining syrup and the freeze-dried coffee. Heat, stirring constantly, until coffee dissolves. Stir in vanilla. Stir pudding and spoon 1/2 can into each of 6 dessert crepes. Fold. Spoon warm Mocha Sauce over crepes. Top with Sweetened Whipped Cream.

Makes 6 individual crepes.
SUGGESTED CREPE BATTER: BASIC DESSERT
SUGGESTED CREPE FOLD: TRADITIONAL

CHOCOLATE MOUSSE

3 1-ounce squares (85 g)
   semi-sweet chocolate
3 tablespoons (45 ml) sugar
2 tablespoons (30 ml) rum
2 tablespoons (30 ml) heavy cream

2 cups (480 ml) heavy cream
2 egg whites
Confectioner's sugar
Chocolate curls

6 crepes

Place chocolate squares in small metal bowl or pan. Set pan in bowl of hot water for about 10 minutes to melt chocolate. Heat sugar and rum over low heat to melt sugar. Add sugar syrup and 2 tablespoons heavy cream to melted chocolate. In a small bowl, beat egg whites until stiff peaks form. (Do not overbeat.) Fold egg whites into chocolate. Beat 1 cup heavy cream until soft peaks form. Spoon chocolate onto crepe, top with whipped cream and place crepes on lightly oiled serving platter. Chill at least 2 hours before serving. To serve, beat remaining 1 cup heavy cream, sweeten to taste with about 2 tablespoons confectioner's sugar, and spoon over crepes. Top with chocolate curls. (To make chocolate curls, warm a chocolate square in 200° oven (93°C.) about 30 seconds. Pull vegetable peeler across top to form curls. Chocolate may need to be reheated after each curl or two).

Makes 6 individual servings.
SUGGESTED CREPE BATTER: BASIC DESSERT
SUGGESTED CREPE FOLD: TRADITIONAL

CHOC-O-MINT

1/2 gallon (2.5 l)
   vanilla ice cream
Shaved chocolate

2 cups (480 ml) Sweetened
   Whipped Cream
Creme de Menthe

8 crepes

Cut ice cream into logs 5 inches long and 1 inch in diameter. Lightly sprinkle crepe with shaved chocolate. Place ice cream log on crepe. Wrap crepe. Top with Sweetened Whipped Cream and drizzle Creme de Menthe across top. Garnish with additional shavings of chocolate.

Makes 8 individual servings.
SUGGESTED CREPE BATTER: CHOCOLATE
SUGGESTED CREPE FOLD: TRADITIONAL

CHOC-O-NUT

1 cup (240 ml) brown sugar
1/3 cup (80 ml) milk
1/4 cup (60 ml) light corn syrup
2-1/2 teaspoons (12.5 ml) butter

1/4 cup (60 ml) peanut butter
1/2 gallon (2.5 l)
   chocolate ice cream
Crushed peanuts

6-8 crepes

Combine brown sugar, milk, corn syrup and butter in saucepan. Heat until sugar is dissolved and butter melts. Remove from heat, add peanut butter. Beat with electric mixer until smooth. Cut chocolate ice cream into logs, 5 inches long and 1 inch in diameter. Place logs on crepe, and fold. Spoon peanut butter mixture over top and garnish with crushed peanuts.

Makes 6 to 8 individual servings.
SUGGESTED CREPE BATTER: CHOCOLATE
SUGGESTED CREPE FOLD: TRADITIONAL

CHOCOLATE VELVET DESSERT

1 package chocolate pudding
1/2 pint (240 ml) heavy cream
1 tablespoon (15 ml) margarine
1 cup (240 ml) light brown sugar

1/2 teaspoon (2.5 ml) vanilla
1 cup (240 ml) hot water
1 tablespoon (15 ml) cornstarch
1 banana, thinly sliced

8 crepes

Prepare chocolate pudding as per directions. Whip heavy cream. Place margarine and brown sugar in saucepan. Cook over low heat until margarine and sugar are well combined and translucent. Add vanilla and hot water. Sprinkle in cornstarch, stirring constantly to combine. Cook over low heat (slow boiling) until mixture coats the back of a metal spoon—about 15 to 20 minutes. Spoon chocolate pudding onto crepe. Place 2 to 3 slices of banana on pudding; fold crepe. Drizzle with caramel sauce and garnish with whipped cream.

Makes 8 individual servings.
SUGGESTED CREPE BATTER: CHOCOLATE
SUGGESTED CREPE FOLD: TRADITIONAL

CINNAMON-NUT COOKIES

2 teaspoons (10 ml) butter
　or margarine
4 tablespoons (60 ml) sugar

1/2 teaspoon (2.5 ml) cinnamon
4 tablespoons (60 ml)
　finely chopped nuts

4 crepes

Spread unbrowned side of crepe lightly with butter. Combine sugar and cinnamon. Sprinkle sugar mixture and nuts over crepe. Roll up and place on baking sheet. Crepes should be at least 1 inch apart. Bake at 425°F. (218° C.) for 5-10 minutes, or until filling is hot and crepes are crisp. Serve hot or cold.

Makes 4 individual servings.
SUGGESTED CREPE BATTER: CINNAMON-NUT DESSERT
SUGGESTED CREPE FOLD: SPIRAL ROLL

COCONUT NIBBLES

3-1/2-ounce can (100 g)
　flaked coconut
1 tablespoon (15 ml) flour
1/3 cup (80 ml)
　finely-chopped almonds
2/3 cup (160 ml) light cream

1 tablespoon (15 ml) honey
1 tablespoon (15 ml) butter
1 egg yolk
Oil for deep fat frying
Confectioner's sugar

10 or 12 crepes

Combine coconut, flour and almonds. Gradually stir in cream. Heat, stirring occasionally, until boiling. Remove from heat; add honey, butter and egg yolk. Spoon about 2-1/2 tablespoons on a crepe and fold for frying. In frypan, fry two or three crepes at a time at 375°F. (190° C.) for 1-1/2 minutes per side, or until brown and crisp. Drain on paper towels. While still warm, sprinkle crepes with confectioner's sugar. Serve warm or cold.

Makes 10 to 12 individual servings.
SUGGESTED CREPE BATTER: DESSERT
SUGGESTED CREPE FOLD: FRY FOLD

COCONUT S'MORES

2 milk chocolate candy bars
    (1.2 ounces (30 g) each)
1/2 cup (120 ml) flaked coconut
1/2 cup (120 ml) chopped nuts

2 tablespoons (30 ml) sugar
1 tablespoon (15 ml) butter
    or margarine, melted
1 recipe Sweetened
    Whipped Cream

6 crepes

Break candy bars into 6 long lengths. Place candy strips, coconut and nuts on crepes, fold tightly and place seam side down in greased baking dish. Sprinkle with sugar, drizzle with melted butter. Bake at 350° F. (177° C.) for 5 minutes, or until chocolate is melted. Serve topped with Sweetened Whipped Cream.

Makes 6 servings.

SUGGESTED CREPE BATTER: DESSERT
SUGGESTED CREPE FOLD: TRADITIONAL

CREAMY LEMON CREPES

2 3-ounce packages (170 g) cream
    cheese, room temperature
2 tablespoons (30 ml) milk
3 tablespoons (45 ml)
    confectioner's sugar

1-1/4 teaspoons (6.5 ml)
    grated lemon peel
Fresh mint (optional)

8 crepes

Stir cream cheese until smooth. Gradually stir in milk and confectioner's sugar, beat until smooth. Add lemon peel. Thinly spread crepes with cream cheese mixture, roll up, and dust with confectioner's sugar. Garnish with mint leaves.

Makes 8 individual servings.

SUGGESTED CREPE BATTER: CHOCOLATE DESSERT
SUGGESTED CREPE FOLD: SPIRAL ROLL

CREPES A LA MODE

The basic dessert crepe and the chocolate crepe lend themselves to a quick dessert when combined with ice cream and fruit filling. Here is a guide to give you some ideas of how to create your own impressive dessert. Remember, these crepes can be made ahead of time. Wrap the ice cream and fruit in them and freeze. When it is time to serve, all you have to do is top with your favorite sauce, nuts or whipped cream.

Crepe	Toppings	Ice Cream	Fruit Fillings
Basic Dessert	Caramel Sauce	Vanilla	Strawberries
Chocolate	Chocolate Sauce	Strawberry	Blueberries
	Sweetened Whipped Cream	Chocolate	Raspberries
		Coffee	Cherries
	Vanilla glaze	Butter Pecan	Cooked apples
	Flavored brandy	Fruit	Peaches
	Flavored liqueurs		Bananas
	Chopped walnuts, pecans, almonds or peanuts		
	Shaved chocolate		
	Crushed peppermint		

CREPES CHANTILLY

1/2 cup (120 ml) toasted almonds 2 bananas, thinly-sliced
1 recipe Sweetened
    Whipped Cream

8 crepes
   Gently fold almonds and bananas into whipped cream. Spoon mixture onto crepe, and fold. Garnish with a dollop of filling.
   Makes 6 to 8 servings.
   SUGGESTED CREPE BATTER: BASIC DESSERT
   SUGGESTED CREPE FOLD: TRADITIONAL

CREPES IN FLAMING WINE SAUCE

1-1/2 teaspoons (7.5 ml)
  grated orange peel
1 tablespoon (15 ml) rum
3/4 cup (180 ml)
  apricot preserves

1 teaspoon (5 ml) honey
1 cup (240 ml) port wine
2 tablespoons (30 ml) Cointreau
  or Grand Marnier
Confectioner's sugar

12 crepes

Prepare crepe batter, adding orange peel and rum. Fold and keep warm. In chafing dish, heat preserves and honey. Add liqueurs, allowing to heat until lukewarm. Ignite. Allow flames to burn out, then spoon liqueur mixture over triangle-folded crepes. Sprinkle with confectioner's sugar.

Makes 4 servings.
SUGGESTED CREPE BATTER: CINNAMON-NUT
SUGGESTED CREPE FOLD: TRIANGLE

CREPES SUZETTE

1/2 cup (120 ml) butter
3 tablespoons (45 ml)
  confectioner's sugar
Peels from 2 oranges, sliced

Peels from 1 lemon, sliced
1 ounce (30 ml) Cointreau
3/4 ounce (25 ml) brandy

8 crepes

In chafing dish, melt butter. Add sugar and stir until smooth. Place orange and lemon peel in butter and simmer until peels become soft — about 20 minutes. Remove peel from sauce and place one crepe in sauce. Allow the crepe to become covered with the sauce. Fold crepe in half and in half again. Move to the side of the dish. Repeat procedure with the remaining crepes. Pour Cointreau over crepes, tilting the dish to allow the liqueur to coat the crepes. Pour brandy over crepes. Ignite the liquid mixture and rotate pan until the flame goes out.

Makes 4 servings of 2 crepes each.
SUGGESTED CREPE BATTER: BASIC DESSERT
SUGGESTED CREPE FOLD: DESSERT

CRISPY COCONUT COOKIES

2 teaspoons (10 ml) butter
  or margarine
1/2 cup (120 ml) firmly-packed
  brown sugar

1/2 cup (120 ml) flaked coconut
1/4 cup (60 ml) raisins

4 crepes

Spread unbrowned side of crepe lightly with butter. Sprinkle with 2 tablespoons brown sugar, coconut and raisins. Roll up and place on baking sheet. Crepes should be at least 1 inch apart. Bake at 425°F. (218°C.) for 5-10 minutes, or until filling is hot and crepes are crisp. Serve hot or cold.

Makes 4 individual servings.
SUGGESTED CREPE BATTER: CINNAMON-NUT DESSERT
SUGGESTED CREPE FOLD: SPIRAL ROLL

DATE-NUT COOKIES

1-1/2 cups (360 ml)
   diced, pitted dates
1/2 cup (120 ml) chopped nuts

1/2 cup (120 ml) water
2 tablespoons (30 ml) brown sugar

12 crepes

Combine dates, nuts, water and sugar in saucepan. Cook, stirring frequently, until dates are softened and liquid is absorbed. Spread about 2 tablespoons filling over each crepe, roll up and place 1 inch apart on baking sheet. Bake at 425°F. (218°C.) for 5-10 minutes, or until filling is hot and crepes are crisp. Cut each crepe into 2 or 3 pieces. Serve hot or cold.

Makes 24 to 36 cookies.
SUGGESTED CREPE BATTER: DESSERT
SUGGESTED CREPE FOLD: SPIRAL ROLL

EASY LEMON CREPES

3-1/4-ounce package (195 g)
   lemon pudding and
   pie filling mix
1-1/4 cups (300 ml)
   pineapple juice
1/2 cup (120 ml) heavy cream

2 tablespoons (30 ml)
   confectioner's sugar
2 cups (480 ml) sweetened
   fresh strawberries, sliced,
   or fresh sliced peaches

8 crepes

Prepare lemon pudding according to package directions, substituting pineapple juice for part of liquid. Cool. Beat heavy cream, adding confectioner's sugar gradually, until soft peaks form. Fold into pudding. Chill 2 hours. Spoon chilled pudding into crepes; fold. Top with fresh fruit.

Makes 8 individual servings.
SUGGESTED CREPE BATTER: DESSERT
SUGGESTED CREPE FOLD: TRADITIONAL

FLAMING APRICOT-NUT CREPES

5-ounce jar (140 g) walnuts
   in syrup topping
16-ounce can (455 g)
   apricot halves, drained

1/4 cup (60 ml) brandy
   or cognac

8 crepes

Empty walnut topping into small saucepan; crush walnuts with fork. Drain apricots on paper towels; cut into quarters. Combine drained apricots with walnut sauce. Heat over low heat until warm. Spoon warm apricot-nut mixture onto crepes, fold, and place in chafing dish. Heat brandy to lukewarm in small pan; ignite, and allow flames to burn out before pouring over crepes. Serve immediately.

Makes 8 individual servings.
SUGGESTED CREPE BATTER: DESSERT
SUGGESTED CREPE FOLD: TRADITIONAL

FLAMING BANANA CREPES

1/3 cup (80 ml) butter
   or margarine
1/2 cup (60 ml) firmly-packed
   brown sugar
1/2 teaspoon (1.5 ml) cinnamon

Dash nutmeg
2 cups (480 ml)
   sliced, firm bananas
1/3 cup (80 ml) rum
1 tablespoon (15 ml) peach brandy

6 crepes

Heat butter, brown sugar, cinnamon and nutmeg in electric frypan. Add bananas and stir gently until tender. Spoon onto crepes, fold, and place in chafing dish. Heat rum and brandy to lukewarm, ignite, and pour over crepes. Allow flames to burn out. Serve.

Makes 6 individual servings.
SUGGESTED CREPE BATTER: DESSERT
SUGGESTED CREPE FOLD: TRADITIONAL

FLAMING COFFEE LIQUEUR CREPES

1-1/2 pint (360 ml)
   vanilla ice cream
1 cup (240 ml) toasted,
   flaked coconut

3/4 cup (180 ml) liqueur

8 crepes

Fold crepes into triangles and arrange around edge of serving dish. Pile small scoops of ice cream in center of dish; sprinkle with coconut. Heat liqueur to lukewarm, ignite, and pour over ice cream and crepes. Allow flames to burn out before serving.

Makes 4 servings of two crepes each.
SUGGESTED CREPE BATTER: DESSERT
SUGGESTED CREPE FOLD: TRIANGLE

FLUFFY CREAM CHEESE CREPES

8-ounce package (225 g) cream
    cheese, room temperature
3 tablespoons (45 ml) heavy cream
Confectioner's sugar
1/8 teaspoon (1 ml) cinnamon

1/2 teaspoon (2.5 ml) vanilla
1 tablespoon (15 ml) orange juice
1/2 cup (120 ml) heavy cream
Melba Sauce, bottled caramel
    sauce or fresh sliced fruit

12 crepes

Stir cream cheese until smooth. Beat in 3 tablespoons heavy cream and 2 tablespoons confectioner's sugar until smooth. Add cinnamon, vanilla and orange juice. Beat 1/2 cup heavy cream until it will form soft peaks. Beat in 2 tablespoons confectioner's sugar, fold into cream cheese mixture. Thinly spread crepes with cheese mixture, roll up, and top with Melba Sauce, caramel sauce or fresh sliced fruit.

Makes 6 servings of 2 crepes each.
SUGGESTED CREPE BATTER: DESSERT
SUGGESTED CREPE FOLD: SPIRAL ROLL

FRENCH SILK CREPES

1/2 cup (120 ml) butter, softened
3/4 cup (180 ml) confectioner's
    sugar
2 ounces (55 g) unsweetened chocolate,
    melted and cooled

1 teaspoon (5 ml) vanilla
2 eggs
1 recipe Sweetened
    Whipped Cream
Shaved Chocolate

8 crepes

In small mixing bowl, cream butter on medium speed with electric mixer. Turn speed down. Add sugar, blend, gradually increasing speed until mixture becomes light and fluffy. Add chocolate, vanilla and one egg. Beat on medium speed for 3 minutes. Add second egg. Beat 3 minutes longer. Chill for 2 hours. Spoon onto crepe. Fold. Garnish with whipped cream and shaved chocolate.

Makes 8 individual servings.
SUGGESTED CREPE BATTER: BASIC DESSERT
SUGGESTED CREPE FOLD: TRADITIONAL

FRUITY CUSTARD CREPES

1 orange
1 pint (480 ml) strawberries,
    sliced
1/2 cup (120 ml) flaked
    coconut

1 tablespoon (15 ml) brandy
1 banana
1 recipe Almond Custard Sauce

6 crepes

Peel orange and cut into sections. Add strawberries, coconut and brandy. Chill. Just before serving, slice banana into fruit mixture and toss. Spoon fruit into crepes, fold, and place on individual serving dishes. Spoon Almond Custard Sauce over crepes. Top with whole strawberries.

Makes 6 individual servings.
SUGGESTED CREPE BATTER: DESSERT
SUGGSTED CREPE FOLD: TRADITIONAL

FRUITY PUDDING CREPES

3-1/8-ounce package (90 g)
    vanilla pudding and pie filling mix
1-1/4 cup (300 ml) milk
1/2 cup (120 ml) white
    grape juice
1/2 cup (120 ml) sour cream
8-ounce can (225 g) peach
    slices, drained

8-ounce can (225 g) pear
    halves, drained
8-ounce can (225 g) pineapple
    tidbits, drained
1/2 pint (240 ml) heavy cream
2 teaspoons (10 ml) sugar
10 maraschino cherries
3/4 cup (180 ml) slivered almonds

10-12 crepes

Combine pudding mix with milk in small saucepan. Cook, stirring constantly, until boiling. Gradually stir in grape juice. Chill 2 hours. Drain fruit on paper towels, dice and chill. Fold sour cream and fruit into pudding. Spoon pudding onto crepes and fold. In small mixing bowl, beat heavy cream with electric mixer. Spoon on crepes. Garnish with maraschino cherries and slivered almonds.

Makes 10-12 individual servings.
SUGGESTED CREPE BATTER: DESSERT
SUGGESTED CREPE FOLD: TRADITIONAL

HELLENIC HONEY NUT ROLL

1/2 cup (120 ml) pecans,
    finely-chopped

4 tablespoons (60 ml) honey
16 paper-thin orange slices

4 crepes

Combine nuts and honey. Spread very thin layer over crepe. Fold. Top with additional honey. Slice each crepe in half. Garnish with paper-thin orange slices.

Makes 8 individual servings of 1/2 crepe each.
SUGGESTED CREPE BATTER: BASIC DESSERT
SUGGESTED CREPE FOLD: SPIRAL

IRISH COFFEE CREPES

1 envelope unflavored
    gelatin
2/3 cup (160 ml) sugar
2 tablespoons (30 ml) instant or
    freeze-dried coffee powder

1 cup (240 ml) milk
2 eggs, separated
2 tablespoons (30 ml) Irish whiskey
3/4 cup (180 ml) heavy cream
Mocha Sauce, chilled,
    or Sweetened Whipped Cream

6 crepes

Stir together gelatin, sugar and coffee powder in small saucepan. Gradually stir in milk. Heat, stirring constantly, over low heat until mixture is smooth. Remove from heat. Beat egg yolks. Gradually stir about half the hot milk mixture into the egg yolks. Return to pan. Heat, stirring constantly, until slightly thick, about 3-5 minutes. Do not boil. Chill until consistency of thick syrup. Add whiskey and beat with electric mixer until light and frothy. Beat egg whites until stiff but not dry; fold into gelatin mixture. Beat heavy cream until soft peaks form, and gently fold into gelatin mixture. Chill until thick, if necessary. Spoon onto crepes, fold, and place on lightly-oiled serving platter. Chill until firm. Serve with chilled Mocha Sauce or Sweetened Whipped Cream.

Makes 6 individual servings.
SUGGESTED CREPE BATTER: BASIC DESSERT
SUGGESTED CREPE FOLD: TRADITIONAL

KEY LIME CREPES

14-ounce can (395 g) sweetened,
    condensed milk
3 egg yolks, beaten
1 cup (240 ml) lime juice

1/3 cup (80 ml) sugar
Green food color
1 recipe Sweetened
    Whipped Cream

6 crepes

Combine milk and egg yolks. Gradually beat in lime juice and sugar until smooth. Tint green. Spoon mixture onto crepes, fold, and freeze approximately 2 hours. Top with Sweetened Whipped Cream to serve.

Makes 6 individual servings.
SUGGESTED CREPE BATTER: DESSERT
SUGGESTED CREPE FOLD: TRADITIONAL

LEMON-GRAPE CREPES

1 teaspoon (5 ml) grated
  lemon peel
1 cup (240 ml) light
  corn syrup

3/4 cup (180 ml) purple
  grape jelly
Lemon peel, cut in
  strips from 1 lemon
1/2 cup (120 ml) butter

12 crepes

Prepare Dessert Crepe batter. Stir in grated lemon peel. Cook crepes as directed. Combine syrup, grape jelly and strips of lemon peel in saucepan; bring to boil. Remove from heat and let stand 20 minutes. Remove lemon peel. To serve, melt butter in electric frypan or chafing dish. Fold crepes in triangles and place in butter. Heat until crepes are warm. Pour warm grape syrup over crepes and serve immediately.

Makes 4 servings of 3 crepes each.
SUGGESTED CREPE BATTER: DESSERT
SUGGESTED CREPE FOLD: TRIANGLE

ORIENTAL PINEAPPLE-RICE DESSERT

1/2 cup (120 ml) cold
  cooked rice
1/4 cup (60 ml) sugar
3/4 cup (180 ml) crushed
  pineapple, drained

1/4 teaspoon (1.5 ml) vanilla
5 marshmallows, cut up
1/2 cup (120 ml) heavy
  cream, whipped
Confectioner's sugar

6 to 8 crepes

Place rice, sugar, pineapple, vanilla and marshmallows into whipped cream. Fold ingredients together. Chill. Spoon onto crepe, and fold. Sprinkle with confectioner's sugar. Garnish with mandarin orange slices.

Makes 6 to 8 individual servings.
SUGGESTED CREPE BATTER: BASIC DESSERT
SUGGESTED CREPE FOLD: TRADITIONAL

PEACH MELBA CREPES

Melba Sauce:

2 10-ounce packages (570 g) frozen
   red raspberries

1/3 cup (80 ml) sugar
2 teaspoons (10 ml) cornstarch
Dash Salt

Thaw frozen raspberries; do not drain. Sieve into small saucepan; discard seeds. Combine sugar, cornstarch and salt; stir into raspberry liquid and bring to boil, stirring constantly. Cool before using.

Filling:

30-ounce can (850 g) peach
   slices, drained
1 quart (960 ml) vanilla ice cream

Sweetened Whipped Cream

8 crepes

Spoon peaches onto crepes; fold. Put 1 small scoop ice cream onto each filled crepe. Spoon Melba Sauce over ice cream and crepes and top with Sweetened Whipped Cream.

Makes 8 individual servings.
SUGGESTED CREPE BATTER: DESSERT
SUGGESTED CREPE FOLD: TRADITIONAL

PEACH SUPREME CREPES

16-ounce can (455 g) peach
   halves, drained
1/2 cup (120 ml) prepared
   mincemeat

1/4 cup (60 ml) chopped nuts
1 tablespoon (15 ml) dry sherry
1/2 teaspoon (2.5 ml) lemon peel
1 pint (480 ml) sour cream

8 crepes

Dice peaches, combine with mincemeat, nuts, sherry and lemon peel. Spoon onto crepes, fold, and place in greased baking dish. Bake at 350° F. (177° C.) for 10 minutes, or until warm. Serve with sour cream topping.

Makes 8 individual servings.
SUGGESTED CREPE BATTER: DESSERT
SUGGESTED CREPE FOLD: TRADITIONAL

PEPPERMINT CREPES

3-1/4 ounce package (90 g) vanilla
    pudding mix
1/4 cup (60 ml) crushed, hard
    peppermint candies

Sweetened Whipped Cream
Canned chocolate
    syrup topping

4 crepes

Prepare pudding according to package directions. Stir in crushed peppermint candy, and chill. Spoon onto crepes, fold, and place on individual serving dishes. Top with Sweetened Whipped Cream and drizzle with chocolate syrup.

Makes 4 individual servings.
SUGGESTED CREPE BATTER: CHOCOLATE DESSERT
SUGGESTED CREPE FOLD: TRADITIONAL

POIRES BOURDALOUE CREPES
(Pear and Almond Cream Crepes)

1 recipe Almond Custard Sauce,
    omitting almond extract
3 fresh pears, peeled
    and halved, or 6 canned
    pear halves, drained
Lemon juice
1 cup (240 ml) red
    Bordeaux wine

3/4 cup (180 ml) sugar
1 stick cinnamon
1 cup (240 ml) crumbled
    macaroons
2 tablespoons (30 ml) Kirsch
    (optional)
1/2 cup (60 ml) red
    currant jelly

6 crepes

Prepare Almond Custard Sauce. Dip fresh pear halves in lemon juice to prevent discoloring (not necessary for canned pears). Combine wine, sugar and cinnamon in saucepan; bring to boil. Add pears and simmer 10 minutes. Remove from heat and cool pears in syrup. Chill. Combine macaroons and Kirsch with Almond Custard Sauce and chill. To serve, remove pears from syrup and drain well. Slice. Spoon some pear slices and custard sauce onto each crepe; fold. Melt jelly and spoon over crepes.

Makes 6 individual servings.
SUGGESTED CREPE BATTER: DESSERT
SUGGESTED CREPE FOLD: TRADITIONAL

POLYNESIAN FRUIT CREPES

1 cup (240 ml) heavy cream
2 tablespoons (30 ml) confectioner's
   sugar
1/2 teaspoon (2.5 ml) vanilla
16-ounce can (455 g) pineapple
   chunks, drained

11-ounce can (310 g) mandarin
   oranges, drained
1 banana, sliced
1 teaspoon (5 ml) rum
1/2 cup (120 ml) coconut,
   toasted

8 crepes

Whip cream, add sugar and vanilla. Reserve 1/3 cup for topping. Gently mix fruit with rum and coconut. Fold fruit mixture into whipped cream. Spoon filling onto crepe, and roll. Top with whipped cream. Garnish with pineapple spears.
Makes 8 individual crepes.
SUGGESTED CREPE BATTER: BASIC DESSERT
SUGGESTED CREPE FOLD: SPIRAL FOLD

RHUBARB-STRAWBERRY CREPES

2 cups (480 ml) rhubarb,
   cut into 1/2-inch
   pieces (about 1/2 pound)
1/3 cup (80 ml) sugar
3 tablespoons (45 ml) water
1/4 teaspoon (1.5 ml) cinnamon

Dash nutmeg
2 teaspoons (10 ml) cornstarch
1 pint (480 ml) sliced
   strawberries, sweetened
1 recipe Sweetened Whipped Cream
1/2 cup (120 ml) chopped nuts

4 crepes

Combine rhubarb, sugar, 2 tablespoons water, cinnamon and nutmeg. Cover and bring to boil over low heat, stirring occasionally. Simmer 5 minutes. Combine cornstarch with 1 tablespoon water; stir into rhubarb, and cook until thickened. Cool. Spoon strawberries onto crepes, fold, and place on individual serving dishes. Spoon rhubarb sauce over crepes, top with Sweetened Whipped Cream and nuts.
Makes 4 individual servings.
SUGGESTED CREPE BATTER: DESSERT
SUGGESTED CREPE FOLD: TRADITIONAL

RICE PUDDING CHIFFON CREPES

1/2 cup (120 ml) white rice
1/2 cup (120 ml) dark
    seedless raisins
3/4 cup (180 ml) milk
1/2 cup (120 ml) water

1/4 teaspoon (1.5 ml) cinnamon
3/4 cup (180 ml) heavy cream
1/2 cup (120 ml) confectioner's
    sugar
1 recipe Sweetened Whipped Cream

8 crepes

Combine rice, raisins, milk, water and cinnamon in 3-quart saucepan. Simmer, covered, until moisture is absorbed and rice is tender. Stir occasionally, adding more water if needed. Chill. Beat heavy cream until it forms soft peaks. Fold into rice. Add sugar gradually to desired sweetness. Chill. Spoon onto crepes, fold, and top with Sweetened Whipped Cream. Sprinkle with cinnamon.

Makes 8 individual servings.
SUGGESTED CREPE BATTER: DESSERT
SUGGESTED CREPE FOLD: TRADITIONAL

SOUR CREAM-RAISIN CREPES

3-1/2 ounce package (100 g)
    butterscotch pudding/pie
    filling mix
1 cup (240 ml) water
1 cup (240 ml) seedless
    dark raisins

1/2 cup (120 ml) sour cream
1/4 teaspoon (1.5 ml) cinnamon
Sweetened Whipped Cream
1/2 cup (120 ml) chopped
    pecans or walnuts

6 crepes

Prepare butterscotch pudding according to package directions, reducing milk to 1-1/2 cups. Cool. Simmer water and raisins together 5 minutes. Drain. Fold sour cream, raisins and cinnamon into cooled pudding; chill. Spoon filling onto crepes, fold, and place on individual serving dishes. Top with Sweetened Whipped Cream and pecans.

Makes 6 individual servings.
SUGGESTED CREPE BATTER: DESSERT
SUGGESTED CREPE FOLD: TRADITIONAL

SOUTHERN PECAN ROLL

1/2 cup (120 ml) butter
1/2 cup (120 ml) light brown
   sugar, packed
1/2 cup (120 ml) honey
1-1/2 cups (360 ml) pecans,
   chopped

2 tablespoons (30 ml) heavy cream
Marshmallows
Candied cherries

6 to 8 crepes

Combine butter, brown sugar and honey in saucepan. Bring to a boil and cook 5 minutes. Remove from heat. Add pecans and heavy cream. Place marshmallows on crepe, spoon mixture over marshmallows and roll. Chill or freeze. Slice into four slices. Garnish with marshmallows and candied cherries.

Makes 24 to 32 pieces.
SUGGESTED CREPE BATTER: BASIC DESSERT
SUGGESTED CREPE FOLD: SPIRAL ROLL

SPICY FRUIT CREPES

1/2 cup (120 ml) dried
   peaches or pears
1/2 cup (120 ml) raisins
1 cup (240 ml) dried apricots
1 cup (240 ml) dried
   pitted prunes
1 stick cinnamon

3 whole cloves
4 cups (1 l) water
2/3 cup (160 ml) honey
Sweetened Whipped Cream
3/4 cup (180 ml) slivered
   almonds

8 crepes

Cut peaches or pears into quarters. Combine fruits, spices, water and honey in large saucepan; bring to boil. Cover and simmer until liquid is absorbed and fruits are tender, about 15 minutes. Chill. Remove spices and spoon fruit onto crepes, fold, and place on individual serving dishes. Top with Sweetened Whipped Cream and almonds.

Makes 8 individual servings.
SUGGESTED CREPE BATTER: DESSERT
SUGGESTED CREPE FOLD: TRADITIONAL

SWEDISH PANCAKES

1/2 cup and 2 tablespoons
  (90 ml) flour
1/2 cup and 1 tablespoon
  (75 ml) sugar

1/3 cup (80 ml) milk
6 eggs
1 teaspoon (5 ml) vanilla
2 tablespoons (30 ml) butter

12-14 crepes

Combine all ingredients in small bowl and beat with mixer until smooth. Use crepemaker pan in place of small frypan. Preheat unit 4 minutes. Pour a very scant 1/2 cup of batter into pan and tilt to coat interior. Fry pancake until edges turn light brown. Gently lift and turn pancake with spatula. Fry second side until lightly browned, about 1/2 minute. Second side will have a mottled appearance. Remove from pan and repeat. Fill pancake with strawberry or other favorite jam. Fold, and top with sour cream.

Makes 12 to 14 individual servings.

SUGGESTED CREPE FOLD: SPIRAL OR TRADITIONAL

TROPICAL MAGIC CREPES

1 tablespoon (15 ml) cornstarch
1 cup (240 ml) water
1/3 cup (80 ml) honey
1 tablespoon (15 ml) butter
  or margarine
4-1/2 teaspoons (25 ml) lime juice

3/4 teaspoon (4 ml) finely
  grated lime peel
2-3 drops green
  food color
1 pint (480 ml) chocolate
  ice cream

4 crepes

Combine cornstarch in 1/2 cup water in small saucepan. Add remaining water and honey. Stir over medium heat until thickened. Add butter, lime juice, lime peel and food color. Chill. Spoon ice cream onto crepes and fold. Pour lime sauce over crepes and serve.

Makes 4 individual servings.

SUGGESTED CREPE BATTER: DESSERT

SUGGESTED CREPE FOLD: TRADITIONAL

YOGURT CREPES

8-ounce container (225 ml)
  plain yogurt

Fruit preserves
Powdered sugar

8 crepes

Spoon 4 tablespoons yogurt onto each crepe, and fold. Top with 1 tablespoon fruit preserves. Sprinkle with powdered sugar.

Makes 8 individual servings.

SUGGESTED CREPE BATTER: BASIC DESSERT

SUGGESTED CREPE FOLD: TRADITIONAL

SAUCES & TOPPINGS

ENTREE
Bechamel Sauce
Cheese Sauce
Dill Butter
Ginger Orange Sauce
Marinara Sauce
Medium White Sauce
Mock Hollandaise Sauce
Mornay Sauce
Mushroom Sauce
Spicy Sour Cream

DESSERT
Almond Custard Sauce
Brandied Apricot Sauce
Creme Anglaise
Orange Blossom Sauce
Sweetened Whipped Cream

Did you know that sauces were created simply to smother the less-than-perfect taste and odor of food in the days when refrigeration was unknown? Fortunately these "disguises" have been developed to such a height of refinement that now the necessity for sauces is no longer with us, their sublime taste makes them an important part of food preparation.

Like crepes, sauces are part of all the cuisines of the world. But, here again, it was the French who brought saucing to its perfection.

Butter sauces, white sauces, brown sauces, tomato sauces, and emulsified sauces such as hollandaise and mayonnaise can all be used as part of the fillings or toppings of crepes.

Starting with a basic white sauce, you can add spices, cheeses, curry, capers, or a dozen other things and create delectable fillings. To the brown sauces you can add wine, spices, tomato paste. Butter, though not really a sauce, can also be used as a filling or topping for crepes. For savory butters (or *beurres composees*) add pounded anchovy fillets, dry mustard, chives, lemon, nuts or even cheeses like Roquefort or Parmesan.

Then there are the dessert sauces and toppings. Try chocolate sauces, custards, creams or fruit toppings to transform your crepes into beautiful endings for a meal.

The sauces on the following pages are included in a number of the recipes in this book. Unless otherwise indicated the entire recipe is called for.

ENTREE

BECHAMEL SAUCE

3 tablespoons (45 ml) butter
3 tablespoons (45 ml) flour
1-1/2 cups (360 ml) milk
1 small onion

4 whole cloves (studded into onion)
1 small bay leaf
1/4 teaspoon (1.5 ml) salt
Pepper

Melt butter in saucepan. Add flour and stir constantly over medium heat for 2 minutes. Remove from heat and gradually stir in milk. Heat to boiling, stirring constantly. Add remaining ingredients and simmer, covered, 20 minutes. Stir occasionally. Remove onion, cloves and bay leaf. Season with additional salt and pepper.
Makes 1-1/2 cups.
Try with seafood crepes.

CHEESE SAUCE

2 tablespoons (30 ml) margarine
2 tablespoons (30 ml) flour
1/4 teaspoon (1.5 ml) salt
Dash white pepper

1 cup (240 ml) milk
3/4 cup (240 ml) grated processed
    American cheese

Melt margarine in saucepan over low heat. Stir in flour and seasonings. Continue cooking until mixture is smooth and bubbly. Remove from heat. Stir in milk. Return to range, bring to a boil, add cheese. Stir constantly until cheese melts.
Makes 2 cups.
Can be used to top many vegetable crepes.

DILL BUTTER

1/2 cup (120 ml) soft butter
    or margarine

1/2 tablespoon (7.5 ml) dill weed
1/8 teaspoon (1 ml) dried mustard

Beat butter. Stir in dill and mustard.
Makes 1/2 cup.
Serve over warm crepes filled with meat or vegetables.

GINGER ORANGE SAUCE

1/2 cup (120 ml) orange juice
1/4 cup (60 ml) chicken broth
1/8 teaspoon (1 ml) ground ginger
1/4 cup (60 ml) water

1 tablespoon (15 ml) cornstarch
3 tablespoons (45 ml) honey
1 teaspoon (5 ml) tomato ketchup
    or tomato sauce

Combine all ingredients in saucepan and simmer over low heat until slightly thickened.
Makes approximately 1 cup.
Spoon over chicken crepes.

MARINARA SAUCE—MILD

2 1-pound 13-ounce cans (825 g)
    tomato puree
2 6-ounce cans (340 g) tomato paste
1-pound can (455 g) tomato sauce
1 quart (1L) water

2 - 1/2 tablespoons (35 ml) parsley flakes
1 tablespoon (15 ml) garlic salt
1 teaspoon (5 ml) salt
4 tablespoons (60 ml) grated
    Parmesan cheese

MARINARA SAUCE—SPICY

2 medium onions, chopped
4 cloves garlic, minced
1 teaspoon (5 ml) salt
1 teaspoon (5 ml) pepper
2 1-pound cans (910 g) whole
    tomatoes

4 teaspoons (20 ml) oregano
2 teaspoons (10 ml) thyme
2 teaspoons (10 ml) marjoram
2 teaspoons (10 ml) basil
16-ounce can (455 gr) tomato sauce
3 medium bay leaves

Combine all ingredients in saucepan, simmer over low heat for one hour or longer. This is a large quantity recipe. After using as much as you need, freeze the remainder or use it in your favorite pasta dish.

MEDIUM WHITE SAUCE

2 tablespoons (30 ml) margarine
2 tablespoons (30 ml) flour
1/4 teaspoon (1.5 ml) salt

Dash pepper
1 cup (240 ml) milk

In saucepan, melt margarine over low heat. Blend in flour, salt and pepper. Add milk all at once and stir constantly until mixture thickens and bubbles.
Makes 1 cup.
Mixes well with meats, fish, poultry and vegetables.

MOCK HOLLANDAISE SAUCE

2 tablespoons (30 ml) butter
    or margarine
1 cup (240 ml) mayonnaise
    or salad dressing

2-3 tablespoons (30-45 ml)
    lemon juice

Melt butter or margarine in saucepan. Stir in mayonnaise and lemon juice. Cook at simmer until hot. Do not boil.
Makes 1 cup.
Good with egg crepes.

MORNAY SAUCE

1-1/2 cups (360 ml) Bechamel Sauce
1 egg yolk
3 tablespoons (45 ml) heavy cream

1/4 cup (60 ml) Gruyere or
    Swiss cheese
2 tablespoons (30 ml) grated
    Parmesan cheese
Dash paprika

Prepare Bechamel Sauce. Beat egg yolk and heavy cream together. Gradually add the Bechamel Sauce to egg mixture, stirring constantly. Heat to boiling over medium heat. Stir in cheeses and paprika. Continue stirring until cheese is thoroughly melted.
Makes 1-3/4 cups.
Excellent over meat and vegetable crepes.

MUSHROOM SAUCE

1 cup (240 ml) finely
    chopped mushrooms
3 tablespoons (45 ml) butter
    or margarine

1 tablespoon (15 ml) flour
1 bouillon cube
1/4 cup (120 ml) boiling water
Salt and pepper

Saute mushrooms in butter. Add flour and cook 1 minute, stirring constantly. Remove from heat. Dissolve bouillon cube in boiling water and stir into mushroom mixture. Stir constantly until thickened. Season to taste with salt and pepper. If desired, sauce may be seasoned with lemon juice, cayenne, herbs or Worcestershire sauce.
    Makes 1 cup
    Sauce is good topping for many meat or vegetable crepes.

SPICY SOUR CREAM

1-1/2 cups (360 ml) sour cream
1 tablespoon (15 ml) horseradish
1/2 teaspoon (2.5 ml) Worcestershire

Salt and pepper
1/2 teaspoon (2.5 ml) lemon juice
1/2 teaspoon (2.5 ml) chopped chives

In small bowl, mix sour cream and horse radish. Add Worcestershire, salt and pepper and lemon juice. Sprinkle on chives.
    Makes 1-1/2 cups.
    Excellent on beef, vegetable and egg crepes.

DESSERT

ALMOND CUSTARD SAUCE

5 egg yolks
1/4 cup (60 ml) sugar
2 cups (480 ml) milk

1/4 teaspoon (1.5 ml) grated lemon peel
1/4 teaspooon (1.5 ml) almond extract
3/4 cup (180 ml) slivered almonds

Place egg yolks, sugar, milk and lemon peel in the top of the double boiler. Cook over gently simmering water until mixture coats the back of a metal spoon. Add almond extract and almonds to mixture. To cool, set in cold water and stir.
    Makes approximately 2-1/2 cups.
    Use for topping on Almendrado.

BRANDIED APRICOT SAUCE

2 cups (480 ml) apricot jam   1/4 cup (60 ml) brandy
1 teaspoon (5 ml) lemon juice

Heat jam until melted and bubbling. Stir in lemon juice and transfer to chafing dish. Heat brandy to lukewarm; ignite and pour over jam. Allow flames to burn out; stir.
Makes 2 cups.
Good with Beignets or as a sauce for ice cream or custard-filled crepes.

CREME ANGLAISE

1-1/2 cups (360 ml) milk   3 tablespoons (45 ml) sugar
1/8 teaspoon (1.5 ml) salt   Almond extract or Cointreau
3 egg yolks

Scald milk in top of double boiler over simmering water. Combine salt, egg yolks and sugar. Stir in small amount of milk, then add to milk in top of double boiler and cook. Stir constantly until mixture is thickened. Cool. Add almond extract or Cointreau to flavor.
Makes 1-3/4 cups.
Good with chocolate crepes

ORANGE BLOSSOM SAUCE

1/2 cup (120 ml) frozen orange   1 cinnamon stick
   juice concentrate,   2 whole cloves
   thawed slightly   2 egg yolks, slightly beaten
1/2 cup (120 ml) sugar   3/4 cup (180 ml) heavy cream

Combine orange juice concentrate, sugar, cinnamon stick and cloves in a saucepan. Bring to boil, stirring constantly, until sugar dissolves. Simmer, covered, 5 minutes. Gradually add part of the hot mixture to the egg yolks. Return mixture to pan and cook until slightly thickened. Do not boil. Cool. To serve, remove cinnamon and cloves. Beat cream until it will form soft peaks and fold into orange syrup.
Makes 2 cups.
Serve with ice cream or fruit-filled crepes.

SWEETENED WHIPPED CREAM

1/2 pint (240 ml) heavy cream   1 teaspoon (15 ml) vanilla
1 tablespoon (15 ml) confectioner's sugar

Chill beaters and small bowl. Add chilled heavy cream. Beat on highest speed of mixer, gradually adding sugar and vanilla. Whip cream until stiff and double in volume—approximately 1-1/2 minutes.
Makes 2 cups.

BREAKFAST CREPES

Canadian Breakfast Crepes
Corned Beef Breakfast Crepes
Crepes Goldenrod
Denver Brunch Crepes
Eggs Florentine Breakfast Crepes
Eggs in a Basket Crepes
Fluffy Cheese Crepes
Fresh Fruit with Sour Cream Crepes
Granola Breakfast Crepes
Hearty Country Style Crepes
Mexican Brunch Crepes
Mock Jelly Omelette Crepes
Pigs in the Blanket Crepes
Scrambled Eggs and Bacon Crepes
Spanish Brunch
Streusel Crepes

GETTING OFF TO A GREAT START . . .
WITH BREAKFAST CREPES

Breakfast is the most important meal of the day because it means exactly that — breaking the fast. When you wake up in the morning you probably haven't eaten for at least eight hours, maybe more. That means your body needs fuel to push up its energy level to get the "engine" running.

Yet many people say, "I never eat breakfast." Perhaps it's no wonder, when you consider that the choices — eggs, cereal, toast — are usually unvarying day after day. Add crepes to the list and you might soon find that breakfast is the favorite meal of the day for you and your family.

It's easy to always be prepared for breakfasts. Make crepes in advance and keep in the freezer, using as needed.

Having company for brunch? Crepes are the answer here, too. Serve two or three different kinds. Add an unexpected touch by including a vegetable crepe in the brunch menu.

Brighten up your breakfasts with a little imagination . . . and crepes.

CANADIAN BREAKFAST CREPES

1/4 pound (115 g) Canadian bacon, diced	6 eggs
1 tablespoon (15 ml) butter	Mock Hollandaise Sauce
	Paprika

6 crepes

In frypan, saute bacon in butter until lightly browned. Prepare scrambled eggs. Spoon eggs into warm crepes. Fold, and top with Mock Hollandaise Sauce. Sprinkle with paprika.

Makes 6 individual servings.
SUGGESTED CREPE BATTER: WHOLE WHEAT
SUGGESTED CREPE FOLD: TRADITIONAL

CORNED BEEF BREAKFAST CREPES

16-ounce can (455 g) corned beef hash	4 tablespoons (60 ml) butter or margarine
6 eggs	Salt and pepper

6 crepes

Saute corned beef hash in 2 tablespoons butter. Spoon onto crepes, fold and keep warm in 250° F. (125° C.) oven. Fry eggs sunny side up in remaining butter, sprinkle with salt and pepper. Top crepes with eggs and serve immediately. Garnish with parsley.

Makes 6 individual servings.
SUGGESTED CREPE BATTER: ENTREE I
SUGGESTED CREPE FOLD: TRADITIONAL

DENVER BRUNCH CREPES

4 eggs
1 tablespoon (15 ml) green pepper
1 tablespoon (15 ml) onions,
    minced

1/3 cup (80 ml) cooked ham,
    cubed
Tomato ketchup or
    hot pepper sauce

Scramble eggs. Saute 1 green pepper and minced onions. Add ham and sauteed vegetables to eggs. Heat thoroughly. Spoon onto crepe. Top with tomato ketchup or hot pepper sauce.

Makes 6 individual servings.
SUGGESTED CREPE BATTER: ENTREE II
SUGGESTED CREPE FOLD: HALF

EGGS FLORENTINE BREAKFAST CREPES

10-ounce pkg. (285 g) frozen
    chopped spinach
6 hard-cooked eggs, sliced

3 ounce pkge. (85 g) cream cheese
    with chives
1-1/2 cups (360 ml) Cheese Sauce

6 crepes
Cook spinach according to package directions. Thoroughly drain liquid. Add cream cheese to spinach and cook over low heat until cheese melts. Spoon spinach on crepes; arrange eggs slices over spinach. Fold crepes and place in greased baking dish. Pour Cheese Sauce over crepes and bake at 350° F. (177° C.) for 10 minutes, or until hot. Garnish with rounds of hard-cooked eggs sprinkled with paprika.

Makes 6 individual servings.
SUGGESTED CREPE BATTER: ENTREE II
SUGGESTED CREPE FOLD: TRADITIONAL

EGGS IN A BASKET CREPES

6 slices bacon
6 eggs
1/3 cup (80 ml) light cream

Salt and pepper
1/2 cup (120 ml) grated
    hard cheese (Swiss)
Paprika

3 crepes
Grease muffin tins lightly with butter. Line with 1/2 crepe and arrange to make basket. Place one strip of bacon at bottom of each basket. Break shell and drop egg over bacon. Spoon 1 tablespoon cream over each egg. Sprinkle with salt, pepper and cheese. Bake at 325° F. (163° C.) for approximately 25 minutes, or until done. Sprinkle with paprika and serve immediately.

Makes 6 individual servings.
SUGGESTED CREPE BATTER: WHOLE WHEAT
SUGGESTED CREPE FOLD: BASKETS

FLUFFY CHEESE CREPES

4 eggs   1/4 cup (60 ml) grated cheese, processed American,
                 cheddar or Monterey Jack

Scramble eggs. Sprinkle with grated cheese. Spoon egg mixture onto crepe. Fold
and place in baking dish. Top with additional cheese and place under broiler until
cheese melts, approximately 2-3 minutes.
   Makes 6 individual servings.
   SUGGESTED CREPE BATTER: WHOLE WHEAT
   SUGGESTED CREPE FOLD: TRADITIONAL

GRANOLA BREAKFAST CREPES

1-1/8 cup (270 ml) plain yogurt   3/4 cup (180 ml) granola

6 crepes
   Spoon about 3 tablespoons yogurt onto crepe, sprinkle 2 tablespoons granola
on each, and fold. Spoon remaining yogurt over crepe. Garnish with sliced banana
sprinkled with cinnamon.
   Makes 6 individual servings.
   SUGGESTED CREPE BATTER: ENTREE I
   SUGGESTED CREPE FOLD: TRADITIONAL

Note: To make single serving, use 3 tablespoons yogurt and 2 tablespoons granola
for filling.

HEARTY COUNTRY STYLE CREPES

1 tablespoon (15 ml) minced onion   2 slices bacon, cooked
1 medium potato, pared and cut   crisp and crumbled
   into 1/4-inch cubes   1 teaspoon (5 ml) chopped parsley
2 tablespoons (30 ml) margarine   4 eggs

6 crepes
   In frypan, saute onion and potato in 2 tablespoons margarine until soft and
browned. Stir in bacon and parsley. Prepare scrambled eggs. Add potato-bacon
mixture to scrambled eggs. Mix and heat thoroughly. Spoon onto crepes, fold, and
top with hot pepper sauce or heated tomato ketchup.
   Makes 6 individual servings.
   SUGGESTED CREPE BATTER: ENTREE II OR DESSERT
   SUGGESTED CREPE FOLD: POCKET

MEXICAN BRUNCH CREPES

3-ounce can (85 g) sliced
   mushrooms, drained
1/4 cup (60 ml) chopped scallion
2 tablespoons (30 ml) chopped
   canned green chilies
1 tablespoon (15 ml) butter
   or margarine

8 eggs, beaten
3/4 teaspoon (3.5 ml) salt
1 cup (240 ml) grated
   Cheddar cheese
1 avocado, peeled and sliced
7-1/2-ounce can (215 g) taco sauce

8 crepes

Saute mushrooms, scallion and chilies lightly in butter in frypan. Add eggs and salt; stir eggs until done. Spoon egg and some grated cheese onto each crepe, fold, and place in greased baking dish. Bake at 350° F. (177° C.) for 5 minutes, or until cheese melts. Serve with avocado slices and taco sauce.

   Makes 4 servings of 2 crepes each.
   SUGGESTED CREPE BATTER: CORNMEAL
   SUGGESTED CREPE FOLD: TRADITIONAL

MOCK JELLY OMELETTE CREPES

Prepare 4 scrambled eggs. Melt 1/4 cup (60 ml) of favorite jelly. Spoon eggs onto crepe. Place 1 tablespoon (15 ml) unmelted jelly on eggs. Fold crepe. Place 2 teaspoons (10 ml) melted jelly over top of crepe.

   Makes 6 individual servings.
   SUGGESTED CREPE BATTER: ENTREE II OR DESSERT
   SUGGESTED CREPE FOLD: POCKET

SCRAMBLED EGGS AND BACON CREPES

6 strips bacon
4 eggs

1/4 cup (60 ml)
   tomato ketchup

Fry bacon crisp and drain. Scramble eggs. Crumble bacon into eggs. Place egg mixture on crepe. Fold and top with heated tomato ketchup.

   Makes 6 individual servings.
   SUGGESTED CREPE BATTER: WHOLE WHEAT
   SUGGESTED CREPE FOLD: HALF

2 tablespoons (30 ml) chopped onion
2 tablespoons (30 ml) chopped green pepper
2 tablespoons (30 ml) margarine
1 cup tomato sauce
1/2 teaspoon (2.5 ml) salt
Dash pepper
1/4 teaspoon (1.5 ml) chili powder
4 eggs

6 crepes

In frypan, saute onion and green pepper. Add tomato sauce, salt, pepper and chili powder. Heat thoroughly. Prepare scrambled eggs. Place eggs on crepe and spoon 1-2 tablespoons sauce over eggs. Fold. Top with additional sauce.

Makes 6 individual servings.
SUGGESTED CREPE BATTER: ENTREE II
SUGGESTED CREPE FOLD: TRADITIONAL

ADDITIONAL BREAKFAST TREATS

1. PIGS IN THE BLANKET CREPES

Wrap fried sausage links in crepes, spiral roll.
Top with maple syrup and butter.

SUGGESTED CREPE BATTER: ENTREE II
SUGGESTED CREPE FOLD: SPIRAL

2. CREPES GOLDENROD

4 hard-cooked eggs
1 cup (240 ml) Medium White Sauce

Remove yolks from eggs. Place egg whites in White Sauce. Spoon onto crepe and fold. Top with additional White Sauce. Press egg yolk through sieve; sprinkle sieved egg on top of crepe. Serve hot.
SUGGESTED CREPE BATTER: WHOLE WHEAT
SUGGESTED CREPE FOLD: TRADITIONAL

3. FRESH FRUIT WITH SOUR CREAM CREPES

Place your favorite fruit or fruit compote on crepe
Fold and top with sour cream.

SUGGESTED CREPE BATTER: DESSERT
SUGGESTED CREPE FOLD: TRADITIONAL

Mix together 1/4 cup (60 ml) brown sugar, 1/4 cup (60 ml) chopped nuts and 2 tablespoons (30 ml) butter. Spoon mixture onto two crepes, layered for additional thickness. Fold, and drizzle with powdered sugar and water glaze.
SUGGESTED CREPE BATTER: ENTREE II
SUGGESTED CREPE FOLD: TRADITIONAL

INDEX